VIETNAM

A History of the War

Russell Freedman

Holiday House / New York

Map on p. viii © Map Resources
Picture Credits appear on page 145

Library of Congress Cataloging-in-Publication Data

Names: Freedman, Russell, author.
Title: Vietnam : a history of the war / Russell Freedman.
Description: First edition. | New York : Holiday House, 2016. | Includes
bibliographical references.
Identifiers: LCCN 2016001051 | ISBN 978-0-8234-3658-3 (hardcover)
Subjects: LCSH: Vietnam War, 1961–1975—Juvenile literature.
Classification: LCC DS557.7 .F739 2016 | DDC 959.704/3--dc23 LC
record available at http://lccn.loc.gov/2016001051

ii: The names of more than 58,000 American service members who died
in Vietnam are inscribed on this wall at the Vietnam Veterans Memorial in
Washington, D.C.

vi: A soldier on defense duty at Phouc Vinh airstrip in South Vietnam

TO JACOB JAGELSKI

ACKNOWLEDGMENTS

I'm grateful to my first readers, Donna Brook and Evans Chan, whose insightful comments on the manuscript are substantial contributions to this book.

Russell Freedman, New York City,
April 10, 2016

CONTENTS

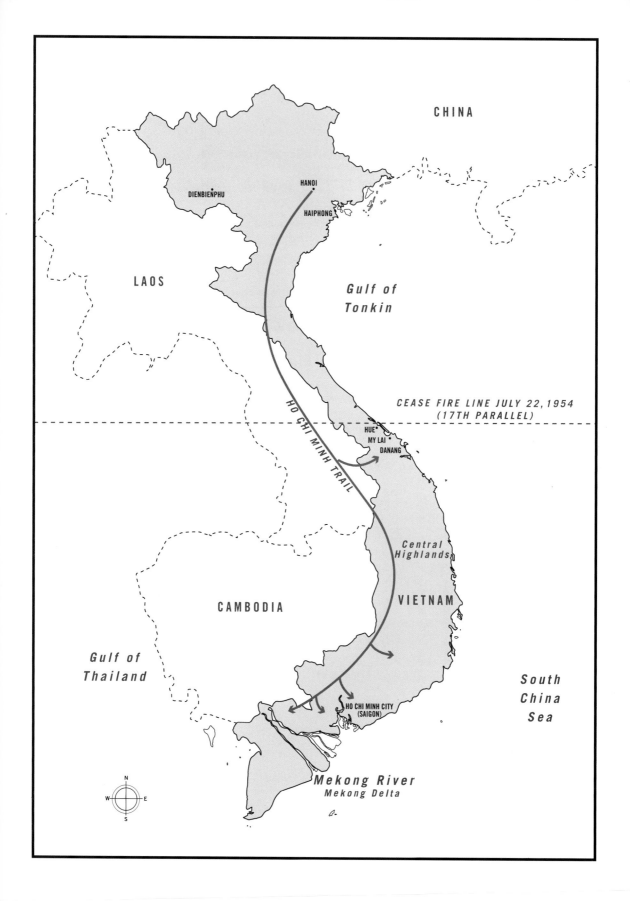

There never was a good war or a bad peace.

Benjamin Franklin

1. The Last Man to Die in Vietnam

America's war in Vietnam was in its seventh year, with no end in sight, when 2,000 decorated veterans staged a four-day "invasion" of Washington, D.C., in April 1971. Wearing their combat medals on tattered military fatigues, they camped overnight on the grassy mall near the Capitol and sang "God Bless America" at daybreak outside the Supreme Court. Then they marched to the Capitol—some in wheelchairs or on crutches because of their war wounds—and, in a defiant act of protest, ripped off the medals they had received for their service in Vietnam and hurled them onto the Capitol steps.

Rarely had the United States witnessed a mass rebellion of this kind among the nation's returning war veterans. Some Americans were outraged.

The veterans had come home from Vietnam with the unsettling conviction that America was fighting a senseless war against a small country that posed no threat to the United States. The Vietnam War, they believed, was killing Americans and Vietnamese without a justifiable cause, damaging America's reputation in the rest of the world and betraying the democratic and humanitarian values that Americans held dear.

Carrying banners and waving flags, 200,000 demonstrators marched at this massive rally in Washington, D.C., on April 24, 1971, to protest the war in Vietnam.

Opposition to the war had been growing steadily since 1965, when the first American combat troops arrived in Vietnam. By 1971, close to 3 million Americans had served in that distant country. Antiwar marches and demonstrations were drawing increasingly angry crowds in cities across America, and yet the carnage in Vietnam continued. A majority of Americans had come to believe that the Vietnam War was a mistake—a disaster in the making.

The veterans' protest marked the beginning of a massive antiwar rally that drew 200,000 protesters to the nation's capital on April 24. Holding blue-and-white placards that read ENOUGH—OUT NOW, the crowd gathered beneath budding trees on the rolling green grounds of Capitol Hill as speakers demanded that Congress stop the bloodshed and end the conflict that had so sharply divided America.

Earlier that week, John Kerry, a decorated twenty-seven-year-old navy veteran of two tours in Vietnam, transfixed the Senate Foreign Relations Committee with his anguished testimony against the war. Kerry had served as an officer on "swift boats," the small, fast aluminum craft used for patrol duties off the Vietnam coast and along the country's rivers. Wounded three times, he had been awarded the Bronze Star and the Silver Star along with his three Purple Hearts. On his return from Vietnam he had become a fierce campaigner against the war. In years to come, he would serve as a U.S. senator from Massachusetts and as President Barack Obama's secretary of state.

In 1971, Kerry was a spokesman for Vietnam Veterans Against the War, founded in 1967 by six veterans marching together in a peace demonstration. Kerry told the Senate hearing that too few lawmakers were willing to take courageous stands against the war, and too many of the nation's leaders were intimidated by a supposed Communist threat in a backward country halfway around the world. He charged that American soldiers were dying to support a "corrupt and dictatorial regime" in South Vietnam. The people of that country, he said, "only want to work in their rice paddies without helicopters strafing them and bombs with napalm burning their villages.

"In our opinion and in our experience," Kerry continued, "there is nothing in South Vietnam that realistically threatens the United States of America. And to attempt to justify the loss of one American life by linking such a loss to the preservation of freedom . . . is to us the height of criminal hypocrisy. It is that kind of hypocrisy which we feel has been tearing this country apart."

Kerry ended his testimony by demanding, "Where are the leaders of our country? How do you ask a man to be the last man to die in

John Kerry receives a medal of valor for his actions
during the Vietnam War.

Vietnam? How do you ask a man to be the last man to die for a mistake?"

John Kerry's words to the Senate aroused intense passions. His testimony was cheered by Americans demanding an immediate end to the war and denounced by the war's determined supporters, who claimed that America's honor was at stake.

Was the Vietnam War a tragic mistake? Or was it, as President Ronald Reagan would claim, "a noble cause"?

2. The Vietnamese: The Long Road to Revolution

When World War II ended in 1945, not many Americans could find Vietnam on a map, and fewer still had ever been there. A small S-shaped agricultural country tucked into a distant corner of Southeast Asia, it stretched along some 800 miles of coastline from China in the north to the Gulf of Thailand in the south. Cambodia and Laos were on the west, the China Sea on the east.

For more than 2,000 years, the Vietnamese had been resisting domination by powerful foreign invaders. As the centuries passed, they fought wars of independence against the Chinese, the French, the Japanese and finally the Americans.

During the first century B.C., the imperial armies of China swept down from the north and conquered the kingdom of Nam Viet, the territory occupied by the Viet peoples. China ruled Vietnam as a colony for the next millennium, despite many bloody revolts.

An uprising in the year A.D. 40 was led by two sisters, Trung Trac and Trung Nhi, who rallied an army that fought and defeated their Chinese overlords. One of the sisters' followers, a woman named Phung Thai Chinh, is said to have given birth to a baby in the midst of battle, yet she continued to fight with the infant strapped to her back.

The Trung sisters set up an independent state with themselves as queens, but just two years later they were defeated by the Chinese. When their rebellion failed, they committed suicide by throwing themselves into a river.

The Vietnamese eventually won their independence from China and established the new state of Dai Viet (Greater Vietnam). As the centuries passed, they expanded their territory, conquering their neighbors to the south. Meanwhile, they kept the Chinese at bay by making tribute payments to the imperial court and fending off occasional Chinese invasions. And they fought among themselves as competing families battled one another in bids for power.

Along the way, the Vietnamese people earned a reputation as skilled and uncompromising warriors. Their centuries of resistance to Chinese domination forged among them a powerful sense of national identity.

"Although we have been at times strong, at times weak," says a Vietnamese proverb, "we have at no time lacked heroes."

During the 1800s, Vietnam faced a new threat to its independence. European powers were carving out colonial possessions in Africa and Asia, where they could obtain raw materials for their factories and buyers for their manufactured goods. In Asia, Great Britain had already conquered and colonized India, Burma and Malaya. French politicians argued that their country could not afford to lag behind. A committee of French dignitaries asked, "Will we be the only ones without possessions in Asia, where the English, Dutch, Spanish and even the Russians are strengthening their position?" France set its sights on Vietnam and its neighbors, Laos and Cambodia, a region the French called Indochina.

French troops storm the citadel and capture Saigon in 1859, beginning the French conquest of Vietnam. From the French journal *L'Illustration,* April 23, 1859.

Vietnam's ruling emperors were too weak to resist French military might. In 1859, the French captured the city of Saigon. They soon took over the rest of southern Vietnam, establishing a colony they called Cochinchina. Over the next twenty years, in the face of fierce resistance, France forced Vietnam to give up more and more of its territory.

Vietnamese peasants feared and hated the foreign invaders who ravaged their villages, looting and killing. Guerrilla bands, armed with swords and spears, often led by Buddhist monks, emerged from hidden sanctuaries in marshes and swamps to attack French outposts. "We have had enormous difficulties in enforcing our authority," the French commander in Cochinchina complained. "Rebel bands

A girl on her way to market walks past cattle grazing on the dike of a rice paddy in this timeless photo of Vietnam's countryside.

disturb the country everywhere. They appear from nowhere in large numbers, destroy everything, and then disappear into nowhere."

In 1883, French troops stormed and sacked Vietnam's imperial palace in the capital city of Hue, destroying the palace library with its ancient scrolls and manuscripts. Later they captured Ham Nghi, the thirteen-year-old emperor, who had taken refuge in a mountain village. Before he fled he had issued a proclamation urging "the rich to give their wealth, the mighty their strength and the poor their limbs so that the country might be rescued from the invader."

The French exiled Ham Nghi, executed most of his followers and quickly installed a more compliant emperor. They followed the old adage "divide and rule" and divided Vietnam into three parts, establishing "protectorates" over Tonkin and Annam in the north and governing Cochinchina in the south as a separate colony. The new emperor was allowed to "rule" from his palace in Hue, but the French were in charge and everyone knew it. "Let us, gentlemen, call things by their name," said the French politician Jules Delafosse. "It is not a protectorate that you want, but a possession."

Colonial rule brought unsettling changes to life in Vietnam. The French controlled the government and the economy. A small number of Vietnamese benefited, collaborating with the colonial authorities and taking advantage of new business opportunities. They became wealthy, spoke French, dressed like Europeans and sent their children to French schools. Traditional temples, monuments and houses that had stood for centuries were torn down and replaced by buildings of French architecture and style. Saigon became known as the "Paris of the Orient," with French police, wide boulevards, luxury hotels and an opera house.

But for most Vietnamese, colonial rule meant hardship and humiliation. Peasants made up more than 90 percent of the population. For generations they had made their living as subsistence

These Vietnamese women were seized and imprisoned by the French colonists after an uprising in 1886.

French soldiers in Indochina, 1888

Leaders of a Vietnamese insurgent army
arrested in 1913 by French colonial authorities

In the Vietnamese countryside, home to 90 percent of the population, farmers planted rice as they had been doing for centuries.

farmers, working small family plots. Many small farmers, unable to raise cash to pay French taxes, fell into debt and had to sell their properties. Large tracts of rich agricultural land became concentrated in the hands of wealthy planters and speculators. Most peasants wound up as tenant farmers, sharecroppers or farm laborers, working plots owned by others. "Oh, the old days when the French were here were very hard," one peasant remembered. "So many people were hungry and did not have enough land. Taxes and rents were too high."

Landless peasants who found jobs at French-owned factories, mines and plantations worked long hours for pitifully low wages. Some were paid in rice instead of money. Conditions were especially harsh on the rubber plantations, where workers were sometimes conscripted at the point of a gun. They were known as "coolies," a derogatory term for Asian laborers. Malnutrition, dysentery and malaria were common on the plantations, and the death rate was high. Runaways, when caught, were executed.

Under French colonial rule, Saigon, as seen in this old postcard, was known as the "Paris of the Orient."

Many French officials knew little about Vietnamese culture and did not speak the language. They believed that they were bringing French culture to a "backward country," that France was destined to "civilize inferior peoples," and they lorded it over their employees and servants. The lowliest French official in the colonial administration earned more than the highest-ranking Vietnamese employee. "The Vietnamese are excellent people as long as they are kept in second place," observed a longtime French colonist.

The bitter pill of colonial oppression encouraged a growing resistance movement. A new generation of Vietnamese leaders, meeting secretly to avoid arrest, sought ways to challenge French rule. Prominent among them was a gaunt, spindly, intense young man with piercing black eyes who called himself Ho Chi Minh. The son of an official at the imperial court, he was one of the privileged few who had received a French education. He had taught for a while in a small village school, and in 1911, when he was twenty-one and eager to see the world, he had signed on as a stoker on a freighter bound for France. He would not return to Vietnam for thirty years.

3. Ho Chi Minh: The Making of a Revolutionary

Ho Chi Minh's early travels took him to the United States. He lived for a time in Boston and New York, working at odd jobs. In years to come, he would reminisce with visiting Americans about his days as a baker at the famous Parker House hotel in Boston.

Toward the end of World War I he settled in Paris, home to a large community of Vietnamese who had served as soldiers and laborers in the French army. Living in a small room in the student quarter, he supported himself by enlarging and retouching souvenir photographs. He attended weekly meetings of a debating society called the Club du Faubourg, wrote a play about a corrupt puppet emperor that was staged by the club and saw enough movies to write articles for the pioneering French film magazine *Cinegraph*. At the same time, he became politically active, joining a group of Vietnamese exiles committed to the struggle against French colonial rule. Rarely without a book, witty and outspoken, "he seemed to be mocking the world," a friend recalled, "and also mocking himself."

In 1919, after World War I ended, leaders of the victorious Western powers—the United States, Britain, France and Italy—met at

Versailles outside Paris to sign a peace settlement with Germany. Ho and his fellow exiles submitted a petition to the Paris Peace Conference, asking the assembled presidents and prime ministers to support the goal of self-determination for the world's subject peoples—a doctrine that had been invoked time and again by U.S. president Woodrow Wilson. The petition was ignored. The Western powers were not ready to give up their colonial possessions. Disillusioned, Ho sought other ways to oppose colonialism.

In 1920, Ho became a founding member of the French Communist Party—the one political party in France that opposed colonial rule. "It was patriotism and not Communism that originally inspired me," he wrote later.

Ho Chi Minh at a meeting of the French Socialist Party, Paris, 1920

Ho had been drawn to the writings of Vladimir Lenin, one of the founders of Soviet Communism. Lenin had condemned colonialism as exploitation of one people by another. Ho became the French Communist Party's leading spokesman on colonial matters. He contributed to the party's newspaper, *l'Humanité*, edited a journal put out by Asian and African nationalists and wrote a political pamphlet titled *French Colonialism on Trial*.

Summoned to Moscow, Ho underwent training as a Communist agent. He was dispatched to the Chinese city of Canton (now Guangzhou), a short distance from Hong Kong, where he worked as a political organizer. It was his job to mobilize Vietnamese revolutionaries who had fled to China to escape prosecution by French authorities.

In 1930, Ho met with a small group of Vietnamese exiles at a Hong Kong stadium during a football match, where they could lose themselves in the cheering crowd and avoid detection by the British colonial police. By the time the final whistle blew, the story goes, they had agreed to form a united Indochinese Communist Party dedicated to overthrowing French colonialism.

A year later, British authorities in Hong Kong arrested Ho during a crackdown on political agitators. He spent a year and a half in a Hong Kong prison before being released. His Communist comrades in Vietnam were not as fortunate. French authorities were determined to crush all anticolonial uprisings. The French army bombed villages suspected of hiding revolutionaries, and French police imprisoned thousands of Indochinese Communist Party members, holding some for years in stifling underground cells. Eventually, 50,000 suspected Vietnamese Communists were arrested and 2,000 were executed.

When World War II broke out in 1939, the Vietnamese faced a new enemy. In Europe, German troops swiftly crushed French resistance and occupied most of France. In Asia, Germany's fascist

A wave of labor strikes and violent uprisings by workers and peasants against the French colonial government took place from 1930 to 1931. This painting at the Museum of the Vietnamese Revolution in Hanoi depicts a confrontation between striking workers and the director of a French-owned rubber plantation, who is ordering them to return to their jobs.

These leaders of the 1930–31 uprisings in Vietnam were among the 2,000 Communists executed by the French colonial authorities.

ally, Japan, moved in to occupy French Indochina—Vietnam and its neighbors, Laos and Cambodia. The Japanese set up military bases, confiscated scarce food supplies and systematically executed anyone they regarded as an enemy. But they left the day-to-day business of governing in the hands of the existing French colonial bureaucracy while Japanese troops swept through Southeast Asia, driving the British from Malaya, the Dutch from Indonesia and the Americans from the Philippines.

The humbling defeat of France at the hands of Nazi Germany suggested to the Vietnamese that their colonial masters were not invincible. And America's entrance into the war, after the Japanese attack on Pearl Harbor on December 7, 1941, raised hopes that an Allied victory would open the gates to Vietnamese independence.

Ho Chi Minh, meanwhile, had slipped quietly back into Vietnam, the first time he had set foot there in thirty years. At a secret meeting led by Ho at a secluded mountainside village near the Chinese border, Vietnamese revolutionaries who had survived the French repression agreed to form the Vietnamese Independence League, better known as the Vietminh. This new group, organized and directed by Communists, would include all Vietnamese political factions, radicals and moderates who were willing to fight both the French and the Japanese. It would emphasize independence as its primary goal and, for the moment, downplay any Communist objectives. And when the time was ripe, the Vietminh would rely on guerrilla warfare to wrest their country from the grip of French colonialism. In a remote mountain hideout, a former history teacher named Vo Nguyen Giap began to train recruits for a guerrilla army. From a twenty-four-man platoon in 1944, the army would grow into a force of hundreds of thousands of soldiers, armed with Soviet automatic weapons.

Japan, an ally of Nazi Germany, occupied French Indochina at the beginning of World War II. Japanese troops are seen here entering Saigon in 1941.

Ho Chi Minh now saw an opportunity to seek American aid. America's wartime president, Franklin D. Roosevelt, had called for self-determination for all peoples and an end to colonialism. As early as 1943, Ho was in touch with American intelligence agents based in southern China. He offered the help of his guerrillas in gathering information on Japanese troop movements and in rescuing downed American pilots. And as the war was winding down in 1945, the Americans came to the aid of Ho Chi Minh.

4. Ho Chi Minh Meets the OSS

In July 1945, as World War II was drawing to an end, a team of American intelligence agents parachuted into a jungle clearing in the mountains of northern Vietnam. As they touched ground and gathered up their parachutes, a crowd of Vietnamese guerrilla fighters came out of the jungle and greeted them warmly.

The Americans were members of the Office of Strategic Services (OSS), the wartime forerunner of the Central Intelligence Agency. Their mission, code-named Deer Team, was to enlist the aid of an unlikely ally—Ho Chi Minh. They wanted Ho's help in rescuing downed American pilots and collecting information about Japanese troop movements. Ho, in turn, had sought the Americans' assistance. He needed arms and ammunition to fight the Japanese occupiers in Vietnam and to oust the French colonialists.

The guerrillas led the OSS agents to a bamboo hut, where they found Ho lying ill and feverish, "a pile of bones covered with dry yellow skin." Deer Team's medic treated him for dysentery and malaria. Ho sent his men into the jungle to search for medicinal herbs. One or maybe both treatments must have worked, because he soon recovered.

Ho Chi Minh (standing third from left) and Vo Nguyen Giap (wearing necktie) pose for a photo with OSS Deer Team agents and Vietminh guerrillas at a jungle camp near Hanoi, August 1945.

The Americans spent two months at the guerrillas' jungle camp. They were not put off by Ho's Communist background, though they didn't know much about him. William Donovan, director of the OSS, had instructed his agents to cooperate with anyone who would work with them against the Japanese, and to steer clear of local politics. Throughout World War II, the United States had sought all kinds of allies, including Soviet Communists, to help defeat the fascist powers, Germany, Italy and Japan. Ho's Vietminh was seen as an umbrella organization of all political factions, Communists among them, that were working for Vietnam's independence.

As Ho recuperated, he engaged in daily conversations with Major Allison Thomas, the Deer Team commander, and with the other Americans. Fluent in English, he reminisced about his travels to the United States and discussed French politics and American history. He put off questions about his own political leanings, saying only that "politics would have to wait until after the liberation of the country." Major Thomas was favorably impressed by the friendly and talkative Vietminh leader. He may have encouraged Ho to expect U.S. support at the end of the war as a reward for his services during it.

Ho's guerrillas were armed with a haphazard collection of ancient muskets and old French and British rifles. The Americans supplied them with up-to-date rifles, machine guns, mortars and grenades. Then they held daily training sessions, showing the guerrillas how to handle the modern weapons and how to maintain them. "The Vietnamese had an uncanny ability to learn and adapt," one OSS agent recalled. "They learned to pull a rifle apart and put it back together after being shown only a couple of times."

Vo Nguyen Giap, the history teacher turned general, was in an early stage of building a Vietminh fighting force. A diminutive man wearing a white linen suit, black shoes and a black tie, he visited the camp to observe the training sessions. "Giap wanted to know why we lobbed the grenade overhand and what activated the mortar,"

General Giap, a history teacher turned guerrilla commander, instructs an early group of Vietminh fighters.

recalled Henry Prunier, Deer Team's interpreter. "One time he looked down the barrel of the mortar. I was shocked. His head could have been blown off."

In 1995, Prunier returned to Hanoi for a reunion with some of the surviving Vietminh guerrillas he had helped. Recognizing him, General Giap picked up an orange, and exclaiming "Yes, yes, yes!" displayed the overhand grenade-lobbing technique Prunier had taught him.

The Americans were still at the jungle camp when Japan surrendered to the Allies on August 15, 1945, ending World War II. At their mountain headquarters near Hanoi, the Vietminh leaders called for a massive uprising to seize power from the Japanese and establish an independent republic. "The decisive hour has struck for the destiny of our people," Ho Chi Minh declared. "Let all of us stand up and rely on our own strength to free ourselves."

The Vietminh had won widespread popular support through its efforts to feed starving peasants during the terrible famine of

A Japanese officer surrenders his sword to a British officer at a formal ceremony in Saigon ending World War II.

During the 1945 "August Revolution," jubilant Vietnamese civilians seized power from the defeated Japanese.

1944–45. Over the next two weeks, during the "August Revolution," General Giap's Vietminh troops, cheered by flag-waving crowds, marched into towns and cities throughout the country. As Japanese troops stood aside, they took over public buildings and assumed control of the government. Vietnamese who had collaborated with the Japanese were dragged from their houses, beaten and in some cases sentenced to death and shot on the spot.

Bao Dai, the puppet emperor appointed by the Japanese, abdicated in favor of the Vietminh. By the end of August, the Vietminh could claim to be the dominant political power in Vietnam.

In Hanoi, Ho Chi Minh met with Colonel Archimedes L. A. Patti, head of OSS operations in Vietnam. Patti's mission was to assist in the orderly release of Allied prisoners of war held by the Japanese.

Patti had met Ho briefly during the Deer Team operation. On August 26, he invited Ho to lunch at his residence. The two men found plenty to talk about. With the defeat of the Japanese and the absence of French colonial forces, Ho saw an opportunity to fill the power vacuum by declaring Vietnamese independence.

As Patti later recalled, Ho hoped to gain American support. He spoke of his admiration for America's founding fathers. He was encouraged, he said, by President Roosevelt's calls for an end to colonialism. And he asked Patti for copies of America's Declaration of Independence and Bill of Rights. A few days later, Ho showed the OSS agent a copy of his own draft for a declaration of Vietnamese independence and asked for Patti's comments.

Some historians argue that Ho was cynically attempting to mislead Patti and manipulate the United States in his bid for political control of Vietnam. Patti believed that the Vietminh leader was sincere. He said later that if the United States had supported Ho's bid for an independent Vietnam, the Vietnam War never would have taken place. "The Vietnam War was a great waste," Patti declared in a 1981 interview. "There was no need for it to happen in the first place."

Henry Prunier, the Deer team interpreter, had mixed feelings. "Ho saw no contradiction between being a Communist and hoping for a democratic way of life for his people," Prunier recalled, adding, "In many ways he was naïve."

With few resources of their own, Ho and his Vietminh comrades badly needed allies in their rebellion against the French. Their neighbor China was embroiled in a bitter civil war as Communists and Nationalists fought for control of the government. The Soviet Union, preoccupied with its position in Europe at the end of World War II, had shown little interest in distant Vietnam. The United States, meanwhile, had championed self-determination for all people. While

Speaking to half a million people packing Bu Dinh Square in Hanoi, Ho Chi Minh reads from the American Declaration of Independence as he proclaims the independence of the Democratic Republic of Vietnam, September 2, 1945.

Ho was an avowed Communist, his lifelong goal was to achieve Vietnamese independence, and to that end he was ready to seek help wherever he could find it.

On September 2, 1945, Ho Chi Minh mounted a hastily built speaker's platform in the center of Hanoi and stood before a crowd of half a million. In an emotional speech, quoting liberally from the American Declaration of Independence, Ho declared the independence of his own new country, the Democratic Republic of Vietnam.

"All men are created equal," Ho announced. "They are endowed by their Creator with certain inalienable Rights, among them are Life, Liberty, and the pursuit of Happiness.

"This immortal statement appeared in the Declaration of Independence of the United States of America in 1776," Ho continued.

"In a broader sense it means: All the peoples on earth are equal from birth, all the peoples have a right to live and to be happy and free."

If Ho expected to gain the support of the United States, he was about to be disappointed. The victorious Allies assigned British forces to occupy southern Vietnam and disarm Japanese soldiers, while Nationalist Chinese troops moved in from the north to oversee the Japanese surrender there. The British and Chinese were ordered not to interfere in local politics. Even so, the British, sympathetic to their fellow European colonists, released and rearmed 1,400 French army troops who had been interned by the Japanese. Then the British stood aside as the French forcibly ousted the newly installed Vietminh government, seizing control of Saigon's public buildings and raising the French flag from the rooftops.

Armed Vietminh guerrilla squads struck back with gunfire and mortars. They attacked the Saigon airport, burned the central market and stormed the local prison, freeing hundreds of Vietminh inmates. Scores of French civilians, caught up in the fighting, were killed.

The French were determined to restore colonial rule. Reinforced by thousands of additional troops shipped hastily from France, they gradually took over most of southern Vietnam. While they could occupy the countryside, they found that they could not hold it. "If we departed, believing a region pacified, the Vietminh would arrive on our heels and the terror would start again," a French soldier recalled.

Chinese troops who had occupied the North, meanwhile, showed no signs of leaving. Fearing that the Chinese were there to stay, Ho Chi Minh and his fellow Vietminh leaders decided that it was better to deal with the French, on condition that they recognize Vietnam's independence.

"Don't you realize what it means if the Chinese stay?" Ho asked his followers. "The last time the Chinese came, they stayed one thousand years. The French are foreigners. They are weak. Colonialism is dying out. Nothing will be able to withstand world pressure for independence. They may stay for a while, but they will have to go because the white man is finished in Asia."

Ho offered to negotiate with the French. In March 1946, France signed an agreement recognizing Vietnam as a "free" state with limited powers within the French Union. French troops were then allowed to replace the Chinese in the North, with the understanding that they would be withdrawn within five years. But disagreements quickly arose over the future of southern Vietnam. France insisted on the establishment of a separate government in the South. Ho refused. Cochinchina, he argued, was an inseparable part of Vietnam. He demanded unification of Vietnam and full independence.

After months of negotiations, the talks collapsed and fighting broke out. In November 1946, French warships bombarded the northern port city of Haiphong, demolishing entire neighborhoods.

Japanese secret police surrender their swords in Saigon, December 13, 1945.

Perched on a Hanoi rooftop, a French machine-gun crew aim their weapon at the street below as the French war to reconquer Vietnam begins, January 1947.

In the center of the city, French tanks rolled over street barricades and French warplanes strafed buildings as the Vietminh fought back with mortars and sniper fire. Refugees carrying their belongings in baskets and on bicycles streamed into the countryside. In December the fighting spread to Hanoi, and the capital city's tree-lined streets became a blood-soaked battleground.

French troops finally drove the Vietminh out of the cities and into mountain hideouts. From a Vietminh camp north of Hanoi, Ho Chi Minh called for a nationwide war of resistance. "All Vietnamese must stand up to fight the French colonialists," he declared. "Those who have rifles will use their rifles. Those who have swords will use their swords. Those who have no swords will use spades, hoes or sticks."

The people of Vietnam would not know peace for the next thirty years.

5. The French War in Vietnam: The Elephant and the Tiger

Alone among the great powers, the United States had equipped and trained the Vietminh guerrillas who were now battling their French colonial overlords. And American intelligence agents had encouraged Ho Chi Minh to expect U.S. support in return for his wartime help. But seismic shifts in global alliances were about to put America on a different path.

The Soviet Union had been a vital wartime ally of the United States, fighting alongside Britain, France and other Allied nations to defeat Nazi Germany. When the war ended, however, the Soviets imposed harsh Communist dictatorships on Poland, Czechoslovakia, Hungary and other Eastern European nations. In so doing, they destroyed their alliance with America, raising fears that Communists planned to expand their rule throughout Europe.

The Soviet Union, a dictatorship ruled by Josef Stalin, was seen as a threat to American values of democracy and free enterprise. Mounting tensions led to the Cold War, the dangerous military rivalry between the United States and the Soviet Union that would last until the early 1990s.

French marine commandos wade ashore on the coast of Vietnam.

The United States responded with the policy of containment, adopted by the administration of Harry S. Truman, who succeeded Franklin Roosevelt as president. The goal was to contain Soviet Communism where it already existed and prevent it from spreading. France, a traditional ally of the United States, was regarded as a critical partner in the defense against Communism. President Truman was reluctant to take any action that might alienate France. So when war broke out in Vietnam, the United States kept its distance, following an official policy of neutrality.

Ho Chi Minh appealed directly to President Truman "to support the idea of [Vietnamese] independence . . . and to take steps necessary to maintain world peace which is being endangered by French efforts to re-conquer Indochina." Ho's cables to Truman went unanswered. He sent similar pleas for help to the leaders of Britain, Nationalist China and the Soviet Union. They also did not reply. "We apparently stand quite alone," Ho lamented. "We shall have to depend on ourselves."

In 1949, the Cold War spread to Asia. The Chinese Communists triumphed in their civil war with the Nationalists, took control of the country and proclaimed the People's Republic of China. A year later, Communist North Korea invaded non-Communist South Korea. The United States and fifteen other members of the United Nations went to the aid of South Korea, while Communist China entered the fighting on the side of North Korea. The Korean War lasted three years, at a cost of 54,000 American lives. Meanwhile, Communist insurrections flared up in the British colonies of Burma and Malaya.

The French war in Vietnam, which began as a struggle over colonialism, was now seen as a battleground in the Cold War. American policymakers began to view Ho Chi Minh not as a Vietnamese nationalist bent on independence, but as a Communist revolutionary, part of a Soviet blueprint for world domination.

By now, France had broken off all contact with Ho Chi Minh and set up an alternative government of its own in the South—the Associated State of Vietnam. The French installed Bao Dai, the former Japanese puppet emperor, as head of this new state, which had limited powers within the French Union. In 1950, the United States and several U.S. allies granted formal diplomatic recognition to the Bao Dai government. The Truman administration abandoned any pretense of neutrality and began to support the French forces in Vietnam with massive military aid.

American foreign policy had shifted from anti-colonialism to anti-Communism.

China and the Soviet Union, in turn, granted diplomatic recognition to Ho Chi Minh's Democratic Republic of Vietnam and pledged unlimited military aid. There were now two rival Vietnamese

French General Henri Navarre meets with Bao Dai,
former Japanese puppet emperor and newly installed
head of the Associated State of Vietnam.

governments—Bao Dai's Associated State in the South and Ho Chi
Minh's Democratic Republic in the North. Bao Dai gained some support among anti-Communist groups in the South, but he was tainted
by having been the puppet emperor of the Japanese. And he could
not rival the popularity among Vietnamese peasants of their "Uncle
Ho," with his promises of land reform, social justice and independence. "No one here respected Emperor Bao Dai," one peasant recalled. "He was just a playboy and a puppet of the Westerners. When
he tried to make a new government, everyone knew it was really the
French behind him."

As French troops and Vietminh guerrillas clashed, the French
were confident that they could easily crush the ragtag Communist
forces. "If those gooks want a fight, they'll get it," French general
Jean Etienne Valluy boasted. He vowed to teach the rebellious Vietnamese "a severe lesson."

The guerrillas knew they had no chance of winning a conventional battle. Instead, they relied on hit-and-run tactics, emerging from their mountain hideouts, striking at French outposts, then melting away. Ho Chi Minh called this the "elephant and tiger" approach, intended to slowly bleed the French and wear them down.

"If the tiger ever stands still the elephant will crush him with his mighty tusks. But the tiger does not stand still. He lurks in the jungle by day and emerges by night. He will leap on the back of the elephant, tearing huge chunks from his hide, and then he will leap back into the dark jungle. And slowly the elephant will bleed to death."

As weapons poured in from China and the Soviet Union, the guerrillas were transformed into a well-equipped modern army, capable of fighting the French on equal terms. By the early 1950s, the

A French patrol questions a Vietminh suspect found "hiding" in the jungle.

French were on the defensive. Vietminh forces controlled most of the countryside in the South, where French authority was limited to narrow bands of territory surrounding the biggest cities. More than 50,000 soldiers from France and the French Empire were dead, captured or missing, and the French public, weary of this "dirty war," as people now called it, was demanding peace.

Sensing victory, Vietminh commanders sought to deliver a decisive blow. Their target was a French outpost in a remote valley in northern Vietnam called Dienbienphu. The French planned to lure the Vietminh into fighting a major battle on the valley floor, where they expected to overwhelm the enemy with their superior firepower.

General Giap, the Vietminh commander, had other plans. His

A wounded Vietminh prisoner receives emergency treatment from French medics.

strategy was to launch a massive assault from high above the valley floor by occupying the mountains surrounding Dienbienphu.

For months, some 250,000 peasant volunteers—called the "long-haired army" because half of them were women—had been trudging through mountain jungles, lugging Soviet-made weaponry to the hills above the fort. Ponderous long-range cannon were disassembled and carried or dragged piece by piece up into the hills. There they were reassembled, camouflaged to avoid detection and protected by antiaircraft guns.

Fifty thousand Vietminh troops surrounded the French fortress when the epic battle of Dienbienphu opened on March 13, 1954. "We had to cross mountains and jungles," a Vietminh soldier recalled, "marching by night and sleeping by day to avoid enemy bombing. We slept in foxholes, or simply alongside the trail. . . . We each had a week's supply of rice, which we refilled at depots along the way. We ate greens and bamboo shoots, picked in the jungle, and occasionally villagers would give us a bit of meat."

The French were stunned that the Vietnamese had managed to haul heavy artillery up onto the ridges overlooking the valley. A Vietminh bombardment destroyed the French airstrip, the fort's lifeline to the outside world. After that, supplies had to be dropped by parachute to the isolated garrison of 12,000 French troops, a risky operation in the face of heavy antiaircraft fire and uncertain weather. Many of the supplies fell into enemy hands.

As Vietminh artillery pounded French positions, infantry troops were crawling closer and closer to the fort through a maze of tunnels. "Now the shovel became our most important weapon," a Vietminh officer remembered. "Everyone dug tunnels and trenches under fire, sometimes hitting hard soil and only advancing five or six yards a day. But we finally surrounded Dienbienphu with an underground

French paratroopers jump from planes in the skies over the besieged fortress of Dienbienphu.

network several hundred miles long, and we could tighten the noose around the French."

The fifty-five-day siege of Dienbienphu became front-page news around the world. Dwight D. Eisenhower, hero of World War II, had succeeded Harry Truman as U.S. president and was determined to prevent a Communist takeover of Vietnam. But Eisenhower's advisers could not agree on what action to take, if any. Some called for U.S. air strikes against Vietminh positions in the hills. A few raised the possibility of using tactical nuclear weapons. But Eisenhower rejected intervention by the U.S. alone. Instead, he appealed to America's allies for "united action" to prevent the "imposition on Southeast Asia of the political system of Communist Russia and its Chinese Communist ally."

Eisenhower's appeal for a coalition of countries to save the French was rejected by Britain, America's closest ally, as being too risky, possibly bringing China into the conflict and triggering a third world war. The United States had just fought a brutal three-year war in Korea, and Congress and the public were wary of any further military involvement in Asia. So Eisenhower increased military aid to the French but, like Truman, ruled out direct intervention.

As Vietminh forces closed in, they played over the radio frequencies of the fort the "Song of the Partisans," the theme song of the French resistance against the Nazis in occupied France during World War II. They wanted to taunt the French defenders that this time *they*, the Vietminh, were fighting for a just cause: *Friend, can you hear the black flight of the crows in the plain? Friend, can you hear the muffled cry of the country being loaded with chains?*

On May 7, 1954, the French were forced to surrender as Vietminh troops overran the beleaguered fortress and raised the red

French soldiers try to survive in the trenches at Dienbienphu as they endure constant shelling from Vietminh artillery in the distant hills.

Victorious Vietminh troops raise their flag over the French
command bunker at Dienbienphu, May 7, 1954.

Vietminh flag over the French command bunker. By then, France
and the Vietminh had agreed to peace talks. They would meet the
next morning at a conference in Geneva, Switzerland.

Eight thousand Vietminh and more than three thousand French
colonial troops, many of them Vietnamese, had died during the
battle of Dienbienphu.

6. Tumbling Dominoes

The Geneva Conference to decide the future of Vietnam got off to a rocky start. The Vietminh, fresh from their victory at Dienbienphu, refused to talk to the French. They declared that they had won the war and earned the right to govern an independent and united Vietnam.

The French, though weary of war and smarting from the sting of military humiliation, were not prepared to give up their privileges and influence in their former colony.

The United States, determined to block the spread of Communism in Asia, agreed to attend the conference only as an observer. Secretary of State John Foster Dulles refused to shake hands with Prime Minister Zhou Enlai, the head of the Communist Chinese delegation. Compromise was possible because China and the Soviet Union were fearful that if the talks collapsed, the United States might intervene directly in Vietnam, triggering a wider war. After two months of difficult talks, the final agreement was hammered out in private meetings between Zhou Enlai and French Prime Minister Pierre Mendes-France.

Vietnam was to be divided temporarily into Communist and

The Geneva Conference to restore peace in Indochina and settle the future of Vietnam took place from April 26 to July 20, 1954.

non-Communist zones. Ho Chi Minh's Democratic Republic of Vietnam would administer the northern half of the country, while Bao Dai's French-backed Associated State of Vietnam would govern the South. Elections to unify the country under a single national government were scheduled for 1956. In the meantime, French troops would withdraw from North Vietnam while the Vietminh pulled its forces out of South Vietnam. The civilian population would be free to settle on either side of the dividing line along the 17th parallel.

This agreement did not please everyone. The Vietminh accepted only after they had been pressured by the Chinese and Soviets to settle for a compromise that required them to give up half the country they felt they had won. The United States, dismayed at the "loss" of

The domino theory warned that if one country fell to the Communists, others would follow like a row of falling dominoes.

North Vietnam to the Communists, refused to endorse the Geneva Accords but pledged not to upset the agreement by force or threat of force.

By now, the United States had raised the stakes in Vietnam. During the siege of Dienbienphu, President Eisenhower had coined the term "domino theory," warning that if Vietnam fell to the Communists, other nations in Southeast Asia would topple as well, tumbling one after another like a row of falling dominoes. After gaining power in Vietnam and the rest of Indochina, according to the theory, Communists would take over Thailand, Malaysia and Indonesia. They might threaten Japan and the Philippines, even Australia.

From then on, the domino theory dominated America's strategic planning. And Vietnam, that small country so far away, assumed enormous importance as the first line of defense in the war against Communist expansion. The United States must prevent "the onrushing tide of Communism from engulfing all Asia," President Eisenhower declared. "No other challenge is more deserving of our effort and energy. . . . Our security may be lost piece by piece, country by country."

7. Ngo Dinh Diem: America's Miracle Man in Saigon

After the Geneva Conference, the Eisenhower administration moved in to take the place of the demoralized French. Emperor Bao Dai, living in exile on the French Riviera, needed a prime minister to govern South Vietnam. American policymakers wanted him to choose a Vietnamese leader they could trust. Bowing to American wishes, Bao Dai appointed Ngo Dinh Diem, an outspoken opponent of French colonial rule and a militant anti-Communist.

Diem had sat out the war with France living in exile in Europe and the United States. He had cultivated a network of influential supporters who believed that he was the right man to head a democratic, independent state in South Vietnam. But he had little support among the South's many political factions. Military leaders saw him as a *tram chan,* someone who "hid under a blanket" to avoid fighting in the war with France.

Some American officials had doubts about Diem. They criticized him as being aloof and out of touch, a career politician who trusted no one except close family members and had little understanding of the needs of the Vietnamese people. He was a devout Catholic in a country that was 90 percent Buddhist. He had the backing of the

Eisenhower administration only "because we knew of no one better," John Foster Dulles explained.

When Diem arrived at the Saigon airport to accept his post as prime minister, few people showed up to greet him. A short, plump, baby-faced figure, he sat in the back of a curtained car as he rode into town, and seemed to have no interest in looking out. "He comes from another planet," a member of his family once said.

The Eisenhower administration underwrote the Diem government with a huge package of military and economic aid. Soon more than 1,500 American military advisers were in the country, helping to train the South Vietnamese armed forces, which were equipped with the latest American weapons.

To bolster Diem's shaky hold on power and undermine Ho Chi Minh's government in the North, the CIA carried out a secret campaign of sabotage. Teams of anti-Communist Vietnamese, trained by the CIA, disrupted public transportation in North Vietnam, contaminated fuel supplies, and spread frightening rumors about the intentions of the Communist government. They recruited fortune-tellers to issue fake forecasts of doom. And they circulated counterfeit leaflets, "signed" by the Vietminh, warning that Catholics faced persecution by the Communists. As a result, nearly a million panicky refugees fled to the South, transported by ships and planes supplied by the United States in an operation dubbed Passage to Freedom. The majority were Catholics fearful of what might happen to them. Resettled in the South, they became Diem's most loyal supporters.

Diem tightened his grip on power by getting rid of Bao Dai. In an election in 1955 that was almost certainly rigged, he claimed to have won 98 percent of the vote. He deposed Bao Dai as head of state and proclaimed himself president of the new Republic of Vietnam.

Diem then refused to go ahead with the 1956 election to unify

Vietnam, called for by the Geneva Accords. Most observers at the time were convinced that if those elections were held, Ho Chi Minh and the Vietminh would be the overwhelming victors. Diem argued that because Communists ruled the North, elections could only be "absolutely free" in the South. The United States backed Diem, saying that the matter "should be left up to the Vietnamese people themselves." North Vietnam's fellow Communist states China and the Soviet Union chose not to intervene.

Diem's Republic of Vietnam claimed to represent the entire country. Ho Chi Minh's Democratic Republic of Vietnam made the same claim. Without free elections, the Vietnamese people were denied the opportunity to choose their political future, and the stage was set for a civil war between South and North.

American Ambassador Henry Cabot Lodge meets with South Vietnamese President Ngo Dinh Diem at the presidential palace in Saigon.

Refugees fleeing North Vietnam wait to board the USS *Montague*, which will transport them to South Vietnam, Haiphong, August 1954.

As president, Diem ruled with an iron hand. He cracked down on the criminal networks that plagued Saigon, and gained a measure of control over the South's turbulent political scene, with its rival factions and warring religious sects. The influential American magazine *Life* hailed Diem as "the Tough Miracle Man of Vietnam." Massachusetts senator John F. Kennedy, soon to become U.S. president, praised South Vietnam as "the cornerstone of the Free World in Southeast Asia."

But Diem's reputation as a miracle man rested on a shaky foundation. The massive American aid that kept him in power was a substitute for his woeful lack of public support. Members of Diem's immediate family, devoted to their own self-interest, held key positions in his regime. Corruption flourished at all levels of the government and among high-ranking military officers who enriched themselves through graft and black marketeering. And Diem had little support in the countryside, where he never fulfilled his promises of land reform.

Under Diem's rule, South Vietnam became more of a police state than a showcase of democracy. Opposition parties were outlawed. The slogan "Denounce the Communists" led to the arrests of tens of thousands of people suspected of being Communists or Communist sympathizers. Suspects were rounded up and imprisoned behind barbed wire in "reeducation" camps. Some were confined for long periods in cramped and inhumane "tiger cages," which were so small that the inmate sat shackled and hunched up, barely able to move. Many political prisoners were tortured and shot, often on suspicion alone, without even a hearing. The head of the secret police, Ngo Dinh Nhu, Diem's younger brother and chief adviser, became the most feared man in South Vietnam.

"Watching a police state in action, particularly an American-financed one, is a sad experience," wrote David Halberstam, the *New York Times* correspondent in Saigon.

By the late 1950s, Diem's campaign to root out revolutionaries had eliminated 90 percent of the Communist movement's members in South Vietnam. "The situation in the South had passed into a stage the Communists considered the darkest of their lives," a Southern activist recalled. "The population no longer dared to provide support, families no longer dared to communicate with their relatives in the movement, and the village chapters which previously had one or two hundred members were now reduced to five or ten who had to flee into the jungle."

Communist Party activists in the South responded to Diem's repression with a terror campaign of their own under the slogan

South Vietnamese soldiers tear down a poster on a village bulletin board that criticizes President Diem. Political opposition was outlawed by the Diem government.

"Extermination of traitors." As a rule, anyone who worked for the Diem government was considered a traitor. Specially trained Communist agents assassinated village chiefs and police appointed by Diem's detested local officials. Their goal, as one terrorist explained, was to "protect the very existence of the [Communist] Party . . . by creating fear in the enemy ranks and by creating faith among the masses in the skilled leadership of the revolution."

In Saigon, meanwhile, a group of eighteen prominent anti-Communist politicians and intellectuals met with the American press at the Caravelle Hotel to present a list of their grievances against the Diem regime: "We can no longer remain indifferent to the realities of life in our country. . . . The people hoped to live in security at last, under a regime which would give them a little bit of justice and liberty. . . . [Instead,] continuous arrests fill the jails and prisons to the rafters . . . public opinion and the press are reduced to silence. . . . Political parties and religious sects have been eliminated. . . . We—without taking into consideration the consequences which our attitude may bring upon us—are ringing today the alarm bell, in view of the imminent danger which threatens the government."

The eighteen signers of the Caravelle Manifesto did indeed suffer the consequences of speaking out. They were promptly arrested.

In November 1960, a group of disgruntled army officers attempted to overthrow Diem. Troops loyal to the president put down the coup after several hours of street fighting that cost 400 lives, including those of many civilians who had poured into the streets to watch the battle. After that, Diem shut himself up in the presidential palace, surrounded by family members and shielded from the growing opposition to his rule. He dismissed criticism of his regime as "Communist propaganda." More and more he relinquished power to his brother Nhu and his glamorous, arrogant sister-in-law, Madame

Nhu, Vietnam's unofficial first lady. She was known to the Americans in Saigon as "the Dragon Lady."

In the United States, preoccupied with the Cold War and the looming threat of international Communism, Diem's trampling of democracy in a small, distant country had not yet become a burning issue. The Eisenhower administration repeatedly urged Diem to make reforms, but his reputation as a strong anti-Communist trumped his failures as a democrat, and Washington did not withdraw its support. In the words of an American official, Diem was "a puppet who pulled his own strings—and ours as well."

In North Vietnam, the Communists secured their grip on power by using many of the same methods as the Diem government—they

Rebel soldiers in Saigon hug the street curb and aim their rifles at the presidential palace during an attempt to overthrow President Diem. Dozens of civilians can be seen watching the attempted coup from a distance.

controlled the press, silenced critics and imprisoned or executed troublesome opponents. Only one political party—the Communist Party—was allowed. Even so, Communists in the North met only scattered resistance. They retained the loyalty of the people by pledging to introduce social reforms, by appeals to patriotism and through the immense influence of Ho Chi Minh, who was admired and promoted as a hero.

Ho's biggest challenge at the time was to feed his people. Years of warfare had devastated the countryside, causing critical food shortages. An ambitious land reform program distributed land to more than half the families in the North, vastly increasing food production and averting another famine. But the reforms, carried out by overzealous officials in charge of confiscating farms and redistributing the land, got out of hand. The campaign resulted in the deaths of thousands of large and small landlords before widespread protests halted the abuses.

Ho found it necessary to issue a public apology for "mistakes and shortcomings." General Giap admitted that "we . . . executed too many honest people . . . and, seeing enemies everywhere, resorted to terror, which became far too widespread. . . . Worse still, torture came to be regarded as a normal practice."

By 1960, Communist leaders in the North had decided that there was no chance for a political settlement in South Vietnam. They were convinced that Diem's repressive rule had alienated so many people that the population in the South was ready to rebel and support the Communist cause.

A military confrontation seemed inevitable.

Meeting in Hanoi, the North Vietnamese capital, Ho and his fellow leaders organized a broad coalition of political groups called the National Liberation Front (NLF) of South Vietnam. Its goal was to

Popularly known as "Uncle Ho," Ho Chi Minh retained the loyalty of his people despite the "mistakes and shortcomings" of the Communist government in North Vietnam. He is seen here visiting a kindergarten in Beijing.

replace the Diem regime with a government that would work toward unification of Vietnam and removal of the American military presence. To that end, the NLF would direct a renewed guerrilla insurgency in the South. The Americans called the guerrillas the Vietcong, or VC, an abbreviation of the words "Vietnamese Communists."

Vietcong forces began to infiltrate back into South Vietnam. Thousands of soldiers carrying tons of weapons and equipment made their way south along a network of primitive jungle paths that snaked through Laos, Vietnam and, later, Cambodia, and would soon

Weapons, ammunition and tens of thousands of soldiers moved from North to South Vietnam along the Ho Chi Minh Trail. Originally a network of primitive jungle paths threading through Laos and Cambodia, the trail gradually developed into an elaborate supply route that funneled military equipment south in truck convoys along highways dotted with rest and service stops and protected by hilltop antiaircraft batteries.

be known as the Ho Chi Minh Trail. Most of the Vietcong soldiers trudging south along this vital supply and communications link were southerners who had moved to North Vietnam in 1954, as required by the Geneva Accords. They were returning now to renew the fight on their home ground.

"Our long-range objective was to liberate South Vietnam," one soldier recalled. "First, however, we had to liberate the nearest hamlet."

8. The Last Days of President Diem

The Communist insurgency in South Vietnam was spreading fast when John F. Kennedy moved into the White House in 1961. Vietcong guerrillas mounted increasingly bold attacks against units of the South Vietnamese army, capturing U.S.-supplied weapons and "liberating" large areas of the countryside from government control.

As the Vietcong saw it, the civil war between the two Vietnams was a continuation of the struggle against French colonialism. They contended that they were fighting a revolutionary war of national liberation. In their view, the French had been replaced by "American imperialists."

President Kennedy and his advisers saw a very different reality. They regarded Vietnam as both a "proving ground for democracy in Asia" and a "test of American responsibility and determination."

Some Kennedy aides urged the president to send combat troops to South Vietnam, as support for the military advisers already there. But Kennedy held back. In place of combat troops, he decided to send thousands of additional military advisers, including 400 Special Forces troops known as the Green Berets, to help train the South Vietnamese army in counterinsurgency warfare. Other

An American military adviser wearing his green beret conducts a training session for South Vietnamese recruits.

advisers would supervise aid projects, set up political education programs and coach the embattled President Diem in ways to reform his corrupt and tottering regime.

In coming to Vietnam, "most American advisers" expected to be received "as members of a more 'advanced' society," historian Frances Fitzgerald has written. "The expectation was not, after all, unreasonable, since the U.S. government sent them out to advise the Vietnamese. But the advisers tended to see themselves in the roles of teacher and older brother, and when the Vietnamese did not respond to them in the expected manner—when they did not even take their advice . . . few saw that the Vietnamese were not the pupils of the Americans, but people with a very different view of the world." While some advisers approached the Vietnamese as equals, others "looked upon the Vietnamese as savages or children with empty heads into which they would pour instruction."

Many of these advisers were idealists imbued with the can-do optimism that had become an American trademark. They arrived with the best of intentions and the belief that American values would win the "hearts and minds" of the Vietnamese and inspire them to rally behind the anti-Communist cause. But very few of the advisers spoke the language or knew much about Vietnamese history or culture or the issues underlying the civil war. All too often, communication floundered in the muddy waters of misunderstanding and misinformation.

By the end of 1963, the number of American advisers in South Vietnam had jumped to more than 16,000. Americans began to take a more active role in the fighting. Helicopter gunships flown by American pilots ferried South Vietnamese troops into and out of

As part of the U.S. effort to win the "hearts and minds" of the Vietnamese, a marine chaplain demonstrates a collection of toys he is about to distribute to a Vietnamese family.

battle zones. American aircraft dispensed herbicides and defoliants in Communist-controlled areas, poisoning food crops and destroying the jungle cover. At times, American advisers accompanied South Vietnamese troops on combat missions.

President Kennedy, like Eisenhower before him, was caught in the cross fire of opposing opinions. Some members of his administration argued against the American buildup. Saving the Diem regime was a hopeless cause, they said. They urged the president to seek a negotiated settlement. Others were convinced that with enough American support, South Vietnam could defeat the Vietcong guerrillas and save the country from a Communist takeover—showing that the United States could be counted on to live up to its commitments as leader of the free world.

American-sponsored projects did not always work out as intended. One effort that turned out to be a disaster was the Strategic Hamlets Program, launched jointly in 1962 by the South Vietnamese army and its American advisers. The goal was to isolate peasants in the South from the Vietcong, and to deprive the guerrillas of the food, shelter and information that villagers often willingly provided.

Millions of peasants were moved, sometimes forcibly, from their ancestral villages to fortified hamlets surrounded by barbed wire, high fences and moats planted with sharpened bamboo spikes. One American adviser, a critic of the program, compared the hamlets to "concentration camps."

Once inside the hamlets, villagers were told that they had to pay corrupt local officials for their new homes, even though the construction materials had been provided free by the United States. Many people ended up having to walk four or five miles to their paddy fields and to the graves of the ancestors they worshipped. And often, the schools and health centers they had been promised

Aerial view of a Strategic Hamlet surrounded by barricades

never materialized because corrupt officials in Saigon pocketed the aid money earmarked for those projects.

Sixteen thousand of these Strategic Hamlets were constructed, but instead of protecting their residents, they offered tempting targets for the Vietcong. And by uprooting villagers from their homes and failing to deliver the promised benefits, they motivated more peasants than ever before to become Vietcong sympathizers.

After two years, most of the hamlets had been abandoned. Vietcong guerrillas controlled more territory than ever, and they were scoring major victories against the South Vietnamese army. At the battle of Ap Bac, a village in the Mekong Delta, a greatly outnumbered Vietcong force mauled a South Vietnamese division supported by U.S. helicopter gunships, fighter bombers and artillery. The guerrillas' heaviest weapons were small mortars. They were subjected to thousands of rounds of rifle and machine-gun fire, to the blasts

A seventy-three-year-old Buddhist monk burns to death after setting himself on fire at a busy Saigon intersection, June 11, 1963.

and shrapnel of hundreds of artillery shells, and to flamethrowers, burning napalm and bombs. Yet the guerrillas stood their ground and humbled a modern fighting force, exposing the inept leadership and low morale of the South Vietnamese army.

Opposition to the Diem regime mounted as crowds of Buddhists and their sympathizers staged protest marches and hunger strikes in several cities. They charged that they were being denied their religious rights while Diem favored his fellow Catholics with key political posts and lucrative business deals. The demonstrations spiraled out of control when government troops threw grenades into a crowd of protestors, killing eight people on the spot and wounding scores of others. Diem ignored Buddhist demands that officials responsible for the killings be punished.

On June 11, 1963, an elderly Buddhist monk sat down on a small brown cushion in a busy Saigon intersection as other monks and nuns encircled him. They doused his yellow robes with gasoline, then stepped back. The monk's hands moved slightly as he struck a match. "In a flash, he was sitting in the center of a column of flame, which engulfed his entire body," a reporter at the scene wrote. "A wail of horror rose from the monks and nuns, many of whom prostrated themselves in the direction of the flames." The monk burned to death while sitting in the lotus position and chanting prayers.

In the weeks that followed, six more monks and a nun set themselves on fire. Diem blamed the suicides on Communists who, he claimed, had infiltrated the Buddhists. He declared martial law. His brother Nhu ordered the secret police to raid the city's Buddhist temples and arrest hundreds of Buddhist leaders. Madame Nhu

Buddhist monks and nuns stage a sit-down protest on a downtown Saigon street after police block their way to a nearby pagoda.

aggravated the crisis when she ridiculed the suicides as a "barbecue." "Let them burn," she told a reporter, "and we shall clap our hands."

News photos showing Buddhist monks consumed by flames shocked people around the world and focused attention on the abuses of the Diem regime. As Buddhist-led demonstrations continued, Nhu's secret police arrested thousands of student demonstrators and tortured many of them. By then, Nhu's own forces were refusing to fire on the crowds, and some were openly encouraging the demonstrators.

"Saigon, those last days of Diem, was an incredible place," an American observer remembered. "One felt that one was witnessing an entire social structure coming apart at the seams. In horror, Americans helplessly watched Diem tear apart the fabric of society more efficiently than the Communists had ever been able to do."

French President Charles de Gaulle called for a new round of talks aimed at creating a "neutral" Vietnam, with a freely elected coalition government with no foreign ties. The proposal was backed by several American newspapers and congressmen. President Kennedy's aides feared that a coalition government would lead to a Communist takeover, but they agreed that the United States could no longer justify its support of the brutal Diem regime. Diem had to go.

American intelligence sources in Saigon were aware that a group of South Vietnamese generals, mainly Buddhists, were planning another attempt to topple Diem. The generals had met secretly with CIA agents to determine if the Americans would support a coup.

In Washington, Kennedy's aides engaged in a heated and sometimes acrimonious debate between those who favored a coup and those who wanted to give Diem one more chance to reform. Without Diem's firm hand, they argued, South Vietnam would collapse into political chaos.

Kennedy was uncertain, and wavered. "My God!" he confided to a friend. "My government is coming apart." He turned for advice to Henry Cabot Lodge, the U.S. ambassador in Saigon. Lodge favored a coup. "We are launched on a course from which there is no respectable turning back: the overthrow of the Diem government," he told Kennedy in a top-secret cable to Washington. "There is no possibility, in my view, that the war can be won under a Diem administration."

In another cable, Lodge summed up the widely held view that "the Viet Cong are steadily gaining in strength, have more of the population on their side than has the [Saigon government]; that arrests are continuing and that the prisons are full; that more and more students are going over to the Viet Cong; that there is great graft and corruption in the Vietnamese administration of our aid; and that the 'Heart of the Army is *not* in the war.'"

Lodge informed the generals that while the United States would refrain from direct involvement, it would not attempt to block the coup.

The end came swiftly. On the afternoon of November 1, 1963, Vietnamese army troops took over police headquarters and radio stations in Saigon and surrounded the presidential palace with tanks. The rebel generals telephoned Diem and offered the president and his brother Nhu safe conduct out of the country if they agreed to surrender. Diem refused. Before the generals could mount an attack, the brothers slipped out of the palace through a secret passageway, carrying a briefcase crammed with U.S. dollars. They entered a waiting car and escaped to a Saigon suburb, where they took refuge in a Catholic church.

The next morning, Diem phoned the generals. "I am ready to resign publicly, and I am also ready to leave the country," he told them. An armored personnel carrier arrived to pick up the brothers.

Despite guarantees that they would not be harmed, Diem and Nhu were shot to death in the back of the armored car with their hands tied behind them as they were being driven to army staff headquarters in Saigon. The rebel generals claimed they had committed suicide.

Madame Nhu was in the United States on a speaking tour when news flashed that Diem and her husband had been murdered in a coup. Refused permission to return to Vietnam, she and her children moved to Europe, where she spent the rest of her life living comfortably in Rome and southern France.

Looking back at Diem's disastrous rule, a veteran U.S. official in Saigon could not conceal his disgust. "For the sake of so-called 'realism,' we abandoned our own principles," he said. "We expected the Vietnamese people to endure a regime that we ourselves wouldn't

Civilians take cover behind an armored vehicle near the presidential palace in Saigon during a battle between rebel military forces and troops loyal to President Diem, November 2, 1963.

A South Vietnamese rebel soldier poses inside the ransacked presidential palace following the overthrow and murder of President Diem and his brother Nhu.

have tolerated for five minutes back home. Maybe morality has a certain place in foreign affairs."

President Kennedy's aides reported that he was shocked and dismayed when he learned that Diem and Nhu had been assassinated. It was not the outcome he had expected.

But the season of violence and assassination was not yet over. Three weeks later, on November 22, 1963, President John F. Kennedy was himself assassinated as he rode in a motorcade through the streets of Dallas, Texas. Vice President Lyndon B. Johnson was riding in another open car just behind Kennedy. He was whisked to the airport by the Secret Service and sworn in as the new president aboard Air Force One while the plane prepared to take off for Washington, D.C.

9. From the Tonkin Gulf to Rolling Thunder

News of Diem's downfall sent jubilant crowds pouring into the streets of Saigon. They tore up portraits of Diem and cheered the army that had toppled him. Political prisoners released from Diem's jails told chilling stories of beatings and torture. In the countryside, peasants destroyed the hated Strategic Hamlets that still remained.

Diem was replaced by a ruling junta made up of twelve generals who pledged to defeat the Vietcong. Ambassador Lodge invited the generals to his office, where he congratulated them. Then he cabled Washington and predicted: "The prospects now are for a shorter war."

Lodge's optimism didn't last long. The ruling generals, greedy for power and inexperienced in governing, proved inept as they succumbed to rivalries and infighting.

In Washington, President Johnson vowed to press forward with the policies of the Kennedy administration. Johnson sent Defense Secretary Robert McNamara on an inspection trip to South Vietnam, where he found Vietcong forces controlling more than half the countryside. In Saigon, the ruling junta seemed paralyzed by indecision and bickering. An alarmed McNamara warned that South Vietnam was facing imminent collapse. It was "my best guess," he told the

Saigon crowds celebrate the overthrow of the unpopular Diem government.

General Nguyen Khanh assumed the South Vietnamese presidency in January 1964 after overthrowing the military junta that had seized power less than three months earlier.

president, "that the situation has in fact been deteriorating in the countryside . . . to a far greater extent than we realized."

In January 1964 the United States threw its support behind another coup, led by an ambitious young general named Nguyen Khanh. The ruling junta was overthrown less than three months after seizing power, this time bloodlessly. Khanh vowed to wage the war against the Vietcong more aggressively. But the new American ambassador, General Maxwell Taylor, complained that the Khanh regime was an "ineffective government beset by inexperienced ministers who are also jealous and suspicious of each other."

President Johnson's military advisers urged him to authorize air strikes against North Vietnam, and if necessary, to send American combat troops. Other Johnson aides advised caution, warning that the growing U.S. involvement in Vietnam might bring Communist China into the conflict, triggering World War III. They wanted Johnson to work toward a political settlement, along the lines of de Gaulle's proposal for a neutral Vietnam. They questioned the idea that a neutral or even a Communist Vietnam would lead to a string of nations across Asia tumbling one after another to Communism. Prominent members of Congress and some of America's closest allies—Britain, Canada, France—joined the appeals for a negotiated settlement that would allow the United States to disengage from what they saw as a hopeless situation.

Through long hours of discussions, Johnson listened to all points

President Lyndon B. Johnson (at right) confers with Defense Secretary Robert McNamara (seated at center) and other advisers after McNamara returned from a fact-finding trip to South Vietnam.

of view. He agonized over the decisions he had to make. The war Johnson really wanted to fight was the war against poverty and inequality in the United States. He hoped to build what he called a Great Society, in which all Americans enjoyed equal rights and access to decent housing, education and medical care. Johnson worried that the growing involvement in the war in Vietnam would drain America's resources and divert attention from his ambitious domestic program.

And yet the president felt that he could not abandon the American commitment to South Vietnam. He could not back down. "If I . . . let the Communists take over South Vietnam, then I would be seen as a coward and my nation would be seen as an appeaser," he later recalled. In Johnson's mind, nothing could be as "terrible as the thought of being responsible for America's losing a war to the Communists. Nothing would be worse than that."

Johnson was determined not to "lose" South Vietnam to Communism. But he wanted "to seek the fullest support of Congress for any major action that I took." So while he resisted calls to unleash a bombing campaign, he increased the number of U.S. military advisers to 23,000. And he approved a secret plan for raids against the North Vietnamese coast by South Vietnamese naval commando units under U.S. control. As the attacks began, fast torpedo boats bombarded Communist radar sites and other coastal installations, while South Vietnamese commandos were landed by sea to blow up rail and highway bridges near the coast.

In August 1964, a strange incident off the northern coast led to a dramatic escalation of America's role in the Vietnam war. President Johnson received reports that two U.S. Navy destroyers had been attacked by North Vietnamese torpedo boats in the Gulf of Tonkin, apparently in retaliation for the sabotage campaign Johnson had approved earlier that year. The American destroyers had been monitoring North Vietnamese radar installations. And yet details about the reported attacks did not seem to add up. Neither U.S. vessel was damaged. No American was injured. And as it turned out, it is doubtful that the second attack, reported on the basis of sketchy radar and sonar readings, actually took place.

Despite the uncertainties, Johnson ordered the first U.S. air strikes against North Vietnam in retaliation for what he claimed was "open aggression on the high seas." And he asked Congress to give him the power to take additional military action as he saw fit.

On August 7, Congress overwhelmingly passed the Tonkin Gulf Resolution, which authorized the president "to take all necessary

This photo taken from the USS *Maddox* shows three North Vietnamese torpedo boats speeding toward the American destroyer during a clash in the Gulf of Tonkin, August 2, 1964.

measures to repel any armed attack against the forces of the United States and to prevent further aggression."

With national elections coming up in November, even opponents of the U.S. involvement in Vietnam felt that they had to back the resolution, which passed after hardly any debate. "Our national honor is at stake," declared Senator Richard Russell of Georgia. "We cannot and we will not shrink from defending it."

Only two members of Congress—senators Wayne Morse of Oregon and Ernest Gruening of Alaska, both liberal Democrats— voted to oppose the resolution. "I believe that history will record that we have made a great mistake in subverting and circumventing the Constitution of the United States," Senator Morse declared. "We are in effect giving the president . . . war-making powers in the absence of a declaration of war. I believe this to be a historic mistake." Many lawmakers concluded later that they had been misled and even lied to by presidential aides who had been "economical with the truth" when providing details of what happened in the gulf.

President Johnson was seeking reelection in November. By ordering air strikes against North Vietnam, and demonstrating that he was willing to use military force, Johnson disarmed his political opponents. He would no longer have to defend himself against Republicans who accused him of being "soft on Communism." At the same time, he promised to keep American troops out of Vietnam. "We are not about to send American boys nine or ten thousand miles away from home," he said, "to do what Asian boys ought to be doing for themselves." When the elections took place in November, Johnson was reelected president by the biggest landslide in American history.

The Tonkin Gulf Resolution provided the legal basis for the air war against North Vietnam, and—seven months later, despite Johnson's campaign promise—for his dispatching of combat troops to South Vietnam. Surrendering its constitutional right to declare war, Congress handed the president a blank check to conduct the Vietnam War as he and his advisers saw fit.

The American air strikes, meanwhile, did not discourage North Vietnam's support for the Vietcong insurgency. For the first time, infantry regiments of the regular North Vietnamese army began to move down the Ho Chi Minh Trail to join the Vietcong guerrillas fighting in the South. North Vietnam appealed to China and the Soviet Union for more military aid, while the Vietcong stepped up their attacks. In November 1964 guerrillas raided an air base at Bienhoa, just north of Saigon, killing five American advisers. On Christmas Eve, the Vietcong bombed a military barracks in Saigon itself, killing two more Americans.

The political scene in the South became increasingly chaotic. Demonstrators protesting the tyrannical rule of General Khanh ri-

On Christmas Eve 1964, a bomb planted by the Vietcong exploded in the garage of the Brinks Hotel, a military barracks in Saigon. The blast killed two Americans and injured 107 Americans, Vietnamese and Australians.

oted in the streets of Saigon, forcing him to resign and flee into exile. Khanh's regime was followed by a succession of weak and deeply unpopular governments. The South Vietnamese army, meanwhile, was weakened by an alarming rate of desertions. Maxwell Taylor, the American ambassador, reported on a "mounting feeling of war weariness and hopelessness" as compared to the Vietcong's "amazing ability to maintain morale," which Taylor considered "one of the mysteries of this guerrilla war."

America's allies wanted no part of the Vietnam conflict. They urged the United States to pull back from a war that the French had already lost and that Saigon could not win. "We are playing a losing game in South Vietnam," Ambassador Taylor warned. Yet Johnson knew he could not simply abandon South Vietnam. "It's just the biggest damn mess that I ever saw," he complained to an aide. "I don't think it's worth fighting for, and I don't think we can get out."

The Communists kept up the pressure. In February 1965, Vietcong troops attacked a U.S. helicopter base at Pleiku, killing eight Americans. This time Johnson struck back by ordering air strikes against military targets in North Vietnam and along the Ho Chi Minh trail in Laos, the Communists' vital supply route.

Johnson and his aides now agreed that the South Vietnamese army could not defeat the Vietcong unless the United States took over most of the fighting. After the attack on Pleiku, the president authorized Operation Rolling Thunder, a sustained bombing campaign that would last from March 1965 to October 1968—America's first major offensive in the war. General William Westmoreland, the American commander, called for two battalions of marines to guard the important air base at Danang. Johnson had once confessed that

A U.S. Air Force Boeing B-52 Stratofortress drops bombs over North Vietnam during Operation Rolling Thunder.

the thought of sending combat troops to Vietnam "makes the chills run up my back." But he felt now that he had no choice.

Senators Mike Mansfield of Montana and Richard Russell of Georgia appealed to the president to "concentrate on finding a way out" of Vietnam—"a place where we ought not to be and where the situation is rapidly getting out of control."

George Ball, Johnson's undersecretary of state and the only member of the administration to recommend immediate withdrawal from Vietnam, warned that the country was "pouring its resources down the drain in the wrong place." But President Johnson, after nineteen months in the White House, had made his decision.

He did not want to be remembered as the first American president to lose a war.

10. The American War in Vietnam

The first American combat troops arrived in Vietnam on March 8, 1965, when two U.S. Marine Corps battalions waded ashore at the coastal city of Danang. Few Americans at the time doubted that the United States, the world's mightiest superpower, could easily defeat a small, backward country like North Vietnam.

"America seemed omnipotent then," recalled Philip Caputo, a young marine lieutenant who led his men ashore that day and later became a noted journalist and author. "The country could still claim it had never lost a war, and we were ordained to play cop to the Communists' robber and spread our own political faith around the world. . . . So, when we marched into the rice paddies on that damp March afternoon, we carried, along with our packs and rifles, the implicit convictions that the Viet Cong would be quickly beaten and that we were doing something altogether noble and good. We kept the packs and rifles; the convictions we lost."

The marines had been assigned to guard the big American airfield at Danang. But they would soon find themselves on the offensive, slogging through rice paddies in search of Vietcong guerrillas.

A month after the marines arrived, President Johnson approved a top secret memorandum expanding their mission by permitting them to be used as active combat troops. In effect, the president agreed to fight a "limited" ground war to back up the ongoing Rolling Thunder air war. Johnson argued that he did not need congressional approval, since he was not actually *declaring* war but simply enlarging the marines' responsibilities.

This controversial "change of mission" was announced to the public in a White House press release that obscured the new combat role of U.S. troops as merely an "increase in effort." Later, historians would say that by taking a series of seemingly small steps, often hidden from the public, the United States became trapped in a quagmire of total commitment to the government of South Vietnam.

That spring, anarchy again overtook Saigon as yet another military junta grabbed power and angry protesters spilled into the streets. In the countryside, the Vietcong dealt a series of crippling blows to units of the South Vietnamese army, which seemed on the verge of collapse. With U.S. ground troops having been committed, there was no turning back, and the American involvement deepened. Troop levels soared. They would reach more than 500,000 within three years.

The United States had taken on the primary responsibility for fighting the war, with the South Vietnamese army reduced to a supporting role. "We were going to share in the fighting," Caputo recalled. "The war would no longer be only 'their war,' meaning the Vietnamese, but ours as well; a jointly owned enterprise."

Supporting the ground troops, U.S. Air Force and Navy warplanes flew daily bombing missions over North Vietnam, Communist-held areas of the South, and the Ho Chi Minh Trail in Laos. By late 1968, American aircraft had dropped a million tons of bombs, rockets and missiles—more tons of bombs than had fallen on Germany, Italy and Japan during World War II—turning Vietnam into the most bombed country in the history of warfare.

Operation Rolling Thunder targeted military bases, fuel depots, ports, industrial sites and infiltration routes. But the air raids failed to stop the steady southward movement of enemy troops and supplies. The Communists moved factories and fuel supplies to remote locations and to underground tunnels and caves. They developed an extensive air defense system, with antiaircraft guns, surface-to-air missiles and radar systems, all supplied by the Soviet Union. During the war, North Vietnam shot down 950 U.S. aircraft and captured 356 American aviators.

President Johnson had ordered that the heavily populated centers of North Vietnam's larger cities be off-limits. Even so, the North Vietnamese dug more than 20 million bomb shelters during the

North Vietnamese high school girls dig their own air raid-shelters in a Hanoi hillside.

course of the war. Propaganda posters urged people to "Call the Shelter Your Second Home." In the words of a popular song of the time, "Our home protects us from wind and fog, the underground shelter preserves our blood and bone."

In Hanoi, there was a shelter every six to thirty feet. Despite the precautions, the bombings inflicted an estimated 90,000 casualties on the North Vietnamese population, including 72,000 civilians.

The goal of the Johnson administration was to force Hanoi to abandon any hope of unifying Vietnam under Communist rule. General Westmoreland declared that the aim of the war was "not to conquer North Vietnam, but to eliminate the insurgency inside South Vietnam."

By gradually increasing the intensity of the bombings, American military leaders expected to break the Communists' morale and force them to plead for peace. But the bombings had the opposite effect. "The Americans thought that the more bombs they dropped, the quicker we would fall to our knees and surrender," a North Vietnamese physician recalled. "But the bombs heightened rather than dampened our spirit."

Testifying before a Senate committee, Defense Secretary McNamara conceded that the bombing campaign had failed to weaken the enemy's will or cripple the flow of manpower and supplies from North Vietnam to the Vietcong insurgents. "Enemy operations in the South cannot, on the basis of any reports I have seen, be stopped by air bombardment—short, that is, of the virtual annihilation of North Vietnam and its people," McNamara said.

Operation Rolling Thunder was accompanied by intensifying ground operations. American infantry patrols engaged in aggressive "search and destroy" operations, seeking to find and annihilate en-

U.S. troops looking for concealed Vietcong guerrillas peer into a South Vietnamese house during a "search and destroy" operation.

emy troop concentrations. Troops plodded across flooded rice fields and followed tangled jungle trails in suffocating heat and torrential rains, drenched in sweat, slapping at mosquitoes, stopping now and then to pick giant leeches out of their boots. They moved along step-by-step, eyes pinned to the ground, examining every rock and clump of weeds, watching for land mines and booby traps that could shear a man's legs off, then scanning the jungle all around, where enemy guerrillas crouched and waited. Ambushes could come from any direction.

To help locate enemy hideouts, American aircraft dropped millions of gallons of Agent Orange and other chemical defoliants on Vietnam's vast jungle canopy, stripping the vegetation bare and exposing concealed Vietcong and North Vietnamese encampments. Once the enemy was spotted, helicopters rushed troops to the battle zone while aircraft and artillery pummeled the area. Powerful defoliants and herbicides were sprayed around roads, rivers and canals, and on crops that might be used to supply enemy troops. Agent Orange was later found to cause cancer, birth defects and other serious illnesses among returning U.S. servicemen and their families, as well as among hundreds of thousands of Vietnamese.

U.S. planes also dropped napalm, a jelly-like substance that burned whatever it touched—trees, buildings, people—turning human flesh to ash. "The napalm hit me and I must have gone crazy," one villager recalled. "I felt as if I were burning all over, like charcoal, and I lost consciousness. Comrades took me to the hospital, and my wounds didn't begin to heal until six months later."

U.S. forces held huge advantages in firepower. The American command declared large areas as "free-fire zones," where anything that moved could be killed, and anything that stood could be leveled. These zones were open to unrestricted artillery and mortar fire

Terrified children run down the road after a South Vietnamese plane
accidentally dropped flaming napalm on their village. Screaming "Too hot!
Too hot!" nine-year-old Kim Phuc ripped off her burning clothing as she ran.
Nick Ut, the Associated Press photographer who took this Pulitzer Prize–winning
photo, rushed Phuc to a hospital and became a lifelong friend. More than forty
years later, married with two sons and living in Canada, Phuc was still being
treated for her agonizing burns.

and to strafing from helicopter machine-gunners. Hundreds of thousands of people fled their homes to escape the shelling and bombing.
The flood of uprooted refugees eventually reached more than 2 million. Civilian casualties, mostly from "friendly fire," were estimated
at about 25,000 dead noncombatants a year.

The Vietcong—called "VC" or "Victor Charlie" by American GIs—
proved an elusive foe. When a firefight was turning against them,
they would pull back and disappear into a maze of underground bun-
kers and tunnels that honeycombed the countryside. After the U.S.
and South Vietnamese forces withdrew, having "liberated" the area,
the Vietcong would quietly move back in.

"You go out on patrol maybe twenty times or more, and nothin', just nothin'," an American soldier complained. "Then, the twenty-first time, zap, zap, zap, you get hit—and Victor Charlie fades into the jungle before you can close with him."

Most U.S. combat troops —"grunts," as they called themselves—arrived in Vietnam with the conviction that the American cause was just. Their fathers had fought in World War II, and now it was their generation's turn to carry the flag. GIs took part in civic action projects designed to win the "hearts and minds" of the Vietnamese people. They built roads, dug wells, dispensed medical care, taught kids to play baseball. Peasants often welcomed American help but still sympathized with the Vietcong.

Because Vietcong troops could vanish into the countryside and mix with the rest of the population, GIs were always on guard. They tended to view all Vietnamese—"gooks" or "dinks" in American slang—with suspicion. An innocent-looking peasant wearing a straw hat and traditional garb might be an enemy soldier about to throw a hand grenade. "You never knew who was the enemy and who was the

A Vietcong prisoner, his arms tied back in a painful stress position, waits to be interrogated.

friend," a marine captain remembered. "They all looked alike. They all dressed alike. . . . The enemy was all around you."

And many Vietnamese in turn, embittered by the bombing and shelling that destroyed villages and ruined crops, resented the overwhelming American presence. Homes were wrecked and sometimes burned or blown up as troops on a search and destroy operation swept through a village probing for Vietcong hiding places.

In his book *A Rumor of War*, Philip Caputo recalls a raid on the hamlet of Giao-Tri: "A phosphorous grenade bursts in a cloud of thick, white smoke, and a hut begins to burn. Another goes up. In minutes,

A South Vietnamese woman, some children and an American adviser sit amid the ruins of a village that was burned to the ground because it was thought to be a Vietcong stronghold. The destruction of Ben Tre, a larger town, for the same reason, resulted in the darkest quotation of the Vietnam War. An American information officer told AP reporter Peter Arnett, "It became necessary to destroy the town in order to save it."

the entire hamlet is in flames, the thatch and bamboo crackling like small-arms fire. The marines . . . are throwing grenades and firing rifles into bomb shelters and dugouts. Women are screaming, children crying. Panic-stricken, the villagers run out of the flame and smoke as if from a natural disaster. The livestock goes mad, and the squawking of chickens, the squeal of pigs, and the bawling of water buffalo are added to the screams and yells and the loud popping of the flaming huts. . . .

"By some miracle, none of the people have been hurt. I hear women wailing, and I see one through the smoke that is drifting across the river. She is on her knees, bowing up and down and keening in the ashes of what was once her home. I harden my heart against her cries. You let the VC use your village for an ambush site, I think, and now you're paying the price."

Search and destroy operations cost the lives of six civilians for every identified Communist killed. "If [the villagers] weren't pro-Vietcong before we got there," said an American soldier, "they sure as hell were by the time we left."

It was a war without front lines. American troops fought again and again over the same patch of ground, conquering territory that could not be held. Major battles took place with North Vietnamese infantry regiments, but most encounters were small skirmishes as American patrols clashed with Vietcong guerrillas. The North Vietnamese suffered heavy casualties—at least half a million of their troops were killed in action. And yet troop replacements continued to move south down the Ho Chi Minh Trail. They were able to fight the U.S. forces to a standoff.

"The thought of compromise in the current struggle . . . seems alien to these men," said an American who interrogated Vietcong and North Vietnamese prisoners. "They see the war entirely as one

A wounded marine is treated by a battlefield medic.

of defense of their country against the invading Americans, who, in turn, are seen merely as successors to the French."

"This being a just war, we shall win," one Vietcong prisoner said. "If South Vietnam is lost, we have got nothing left to live for. We would rather be dead than live as slaves. . . . We are not fighting here to have a cease-fire and prolonged division. It is the Americans who sent their troops here. They will have to make the decision to leave. Nobody can make it for them."

11. The Antiwar Movement

As the war heated up, so did the controversies swirling around it. Supporters of the war, the "hawks," demanded tougher military action. They wanted the president to send more troops and to intensify the bombing. Opponents of the war, the "doves," urged a negotiated settlement and eventual U.S. withdrawal.

At first, big majorities in Congress and much of the American public backed President Johnson's war policies. But as American casualties mounted, public opinion changed. Support for the war plunged. Antiwar activism increased dramatically.

During World War II, Americans had rallied as a united people. Now the country was sharply divided. Increasing numbers of Americans questioned the judgment of their leaders and the foreign policy decisions of their government. By the end of 1967, according to polls, a majority of Americans believed that the Vietnam War was a mistake.

"It was a time of turbulence on the one hand, but also a period in which citizenship took on the form of real action," one war protester recalled. "It was an absolute moral choice that people took."

The growing antiwar movement embraced hundreds of political

'CHOPPING BLOCK'

This 1970 political cartoon suggests the impact of the Vietnam War on American public opinion.

action groups with widely differing points of view—among them, flower-power hippies, political radicals, mainstream liberals, and a group called Vietnam Veterans Against the War. They believed that by backing a corrupt and authoritarian government, the United States was betraying its own democratic values. And they were dismayed by the spectacle of an industrial superpower raining bombs on a backward peasant country. America's involvement, they argued, would bring only death and destruction to Vietnam, not a victory for democracy.

Social activists and civil-rights leaders lashed out against a conflict that was distracting the nation from the president's Great Society domestic reform proposals and his unfinished civil-rights agenda. "The Great Society has been shot down on the battlefields of Vietnam," Dr. Martin Luther King Jr. declared. "The suffering poor of

Martin Luther King Jr. speaks against the Vietnam War at the University of Minnesota, April 27, 1967.

Vietnam and the poor of America are paying the double price of smashed hopes at home and death and corruption in Vietnam."

On American college campuses, students and professors organized "teach-ins"—debates, lectures, movies and musical events aimed at protesting the war. And in cities across the country, speakers denounced the war as thousands of protesters demonstrated and marched.

More than half a million young men resisted the draft. Some refused to register. Others burned their draft cards in widely reported public ceremonies. About 50,000 draft resisters escaped prosecution by fleeing to Canada, Sweden and other countries.

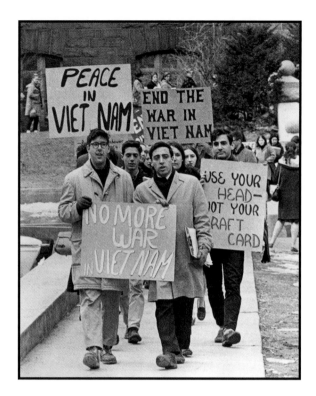

Student protesters at the University of Wisconsin in Madison

Protesters charged that the draft was unfair. Minorities and the poor were four times as likely to be called up and see combat in Vietnam as young men from affluent middle-class families who could afford to go to college and obtain student deferments. The sons of officials waging the war rarely saw any fighting. "The great majority of [draftees] are fresh out of high school, or off the farm or the production lines," *Newsweek* magazine reported.

The first major antiwar rally in the nation's capital took place on April 17, 1965—just a month after the first combat troops had landed at Danang. About 16,000 people picketed the White House and marched on the Capitol, singing peace songs and carrying signs that read NO MORE WAR and WE WANT PEACE NOW.

As the war dragged on, the demonstrations grew larger and the protesters more angry. Antiwar marchers surged through the streets denouncing the president, shouting, "Hey, hey, LBJ, how many kids did you kill today?"

On October 21, 1967, a crowd estimated at 50,000 gathered at the Lincoln Memorial in Washington. By then, more than 13,000 Americans had been killed in Vietnam and 86,000 wounded. After a long day of speeches, 35,000 of the protesters marched to the Pentagon, where they confronted rows of armed soldiers guarding the site. Hippies in fanciful garb pressed forward to place flowers in the barrels of soldiers' bayonet-tipped rifles. "Will you take my flower?" asked a dancing girl. "Please do take my flower. Are you afraid of flowers?"

Violence flared when impulsive protesters, vowing to shut down the Pentagon, attempted to storm the entrance to the building. They were driven back by the rifle butts of soldiers and nightsticks of federal marshals. Demonstrators threw bottles and eggs. Several tear-gas canisters exploded outside the building, and the Pentagon steps were spattered with blood. By the time the crowd dispersed, 682

A young man wearing a helmet with a peace sign burns his draft card during a demonstration at Selective Service headquarters in Washington, D.C.

An antiwar demonstrator offers a flower to a military policeman on guard at the Pentagon.

people had been arrested, among them the novelist Norman Mailer and the famous authority on child care Dr. Benjamin Spock.

President Johnson was convinced that antiwar protesters were encouraging the Vietcong and undermining the American cause. He ordered the CIA to begin a secret (and illegal) domestic spying project, Operation Chaos, to determine foreign influences, if any, on the antiwar movement. Aimed originally at protest leaders, Operation Chaos eventually collected information on 300,000 Americans. But the CIA later reported that no significant foreign influences were ever found.

Military leaders continued to insist that the United States was winning the war. "We are steadily winning it," the U.S. command in Saigon reported, "and the pace accelerates as we reinforce our successes and intensify our pressures."

General Westmoreland pursued an "attrition" strategy designed to wear down the Communists by inflicting such heavy losses that they would lose the will and ability to wage war. The main measure of success was the body count—how many of the enemy had been killed during a given period of time. Since any innocent-looking peasant might be a guerrilla or a guerrilla sympathizer, civilians killed during bombings or shellings were often included in the body count, along with dead guerrillas.

By late 1967, Westmoreland was claiming that enemy forces were being destroyed faster than they could be replaced. He reassured the American public that the war was going well, declaring, "We have reached an important point where the end begins to come into view."

But increasingly, high-ranking officials in the Johnson administration had their doubts and did not hesitate to express them. Defense Secretary McNamara, who had once urged escalation, was now disillusioned. He argued in favor of negotiations and a compromise settlement, and called for a halt to the bombing, which was not producing the intended results. "The picture of the world's greatest superpower killing or seriously injuring 1,000 noncombatants a week, while trying to pound a tiny, backward nation into submission on an issue whose merits are hotly disputed, is not a pretty one," he later wrote.

Protesting the Vietnam War in Washington, D.C., October 21, 1967

A Vietnam veteran wearing a Purple Heart medal watches a peace march in San Francisco, April 1967.

In Hanoi, North Vietnam's leaders were also engaged in a bitter dispute over the course of the war. One group, concerned about the mounting toll of death and destruction, wanted to seek a negotiated settlement. Another faction urged an all-out offensive that would inspire popular uprisings in the South and bring the tottering Saigon government to its knees.

The North Vietnamese opted for a surprise offensive, to be launched during the Lunar New Year holiday of Tet.

12. The Tet Offensive

Before daybreak on January 31, 1968, as the Year of the Monkey began, a squad of nineteen Vietcong commandos blew a hole in the wall surrounding the U.S. embassy in Saigon and fought a six-hour battle with marine guards—a firefight witnessed by millions of Americans on television. Other Vietcong units occupied the national radio station and assaulted the Saigon airport and the presidential palace before being driven off. Throughout South Vietnam, meanwhile, some 70,000 North Vietnamese infantry troops and Vietcong guerrillas attacked more than a hundred cities, towns and military bases.

Some of the most savage fighting took place in the old imperial capital of Hue, a once-lovely city of temples and palaces on the Perfume River and an important cultural and religious center. During the battle for Hue, one of the longest and bloodiest of the war, bombing and shelling destroyed many of the ancient city's historic buildings and monuments.

As the Tet Offensive began, North Vietnamese forces seized control of Hue, set up a new government and systematically eliminated political opponents. As many as 3,000 Vietnamese who

Residents of Cholon, the Chinese section of Saigon, sift through the ruins of their homes after surprise attacks by Vietcong guerrillas at the start of the Tet Offensive, February 1968.

had worked for the Saigon government or for the Americans were executed, along with foreigners suspected of being spies. Most of the victims tried to hide and some managed to flee, but many were captured in their homes. They were marched down the deserted streets, their arms bound behind their backs, to prisoner collection points outside the city, where they were shot.

American marines and South Vietnamese army units counterattacked. They recaptured Hue after a month of brutal block-by-block, house-to-house combat. "My first impression was of desolation, utter devastation," remembered Myron Harrington, who commanded a marine company that entered the devastated city. "There were burnt-out tanks and trucks, and upturned automobiles still smoldering. Bodies lay everywhere, most of them civilians. The smoke and stench blended, like in some kind of horror movie—except that it lacked weird music."

"There had been some reluctance about bombing the [old imperial] palace," Michael Herr reported, "but a lot of the bombing nearby had done heavy damage, and there had been some shelling, too. The large bronze urns were dented beyond repairing, and the rain poured through a hole in the roof of the throne room, soaking the two small thrones where the [Vietnamese] royalty had sat . . . A heavy dust covered everything. The crown of the main gate had collapsed, and in the garden the broken branches of the old cay-dai trees lay like the forms of giant insects seared in a fire, wispy, delicate, dead."

After the North Vietnamese and Vietcong forces retreated, the South Vietnamese army rounded up and executed hundreds of civilians in Hue who were suspected of collaborating with the enemy. Their bodies were thrown into the common graves that held the victims of the Vietcong. Twenty years of terrorism and civil war had

A U.S. Marine's troops in the damaged Imperial Palace during the battle for Hue.

left a bitter legacy. "Communists and [Saigon] forces alike considered ruthlessness a necessity if not a virtue," Philip Caputo wrote. "Whether committed in the name of principles or out of vengeance, atrocities were as common to the Vietnamese battlefields as shell craters and barbed wire."

Outside Hue and other cities in the South, battles were fought over hundreds of villages and hamlets and at remote military bases. Khesanh was an isolated U.S. Marine base near the North Vietnamese border. A massive force of 40,000 North Vietnamese and Vietcong infantry troops besieged the base, manned by 6,000 marines. Although Khesanh by itself had little strategic value, it became a symbol of U.S. determination when the Pentagon ordered that it be held "at all costs." To President Johnson and other Americans, the siege was a cautionary reminder of the Vietminh encirclement of the French at Dienbienphu.

The marines relied for defense on long-range artillery and B-52 bombers, which unloaded a record 75,000 tons of explosives on the surrounding enemy troops. Helicopters and cargo planes, flying over "terrain like moonscapes, cratered and pitted and full of skilled North Vietnamese gunners," dropped supplies and troop replacements to the base and evacuated the wounded. At least 10,000 enemy troops lost their lives under the downpour of bombs, napalm and artillery shells during the nine-week siege. Fewer than 500 marines were killed in action, and the base held out. The North Vietnamese and Vietcong forces pulled back, but they had succeeded in drawing the Americans to a remote area while they were attacking South Vietnam's cities and towns.

General Westmoreland saw the war as an opportunity to test new weapons and tactics. During the siege of Khesanh, he raised the possibility of using "tactical nuclear weapons or chemical agents" if the

Besieged by enemy troops in the surrounding hills, U.S. Marines at Khesanh fire an M107—a 75-mm self-propelled, lightweight, long-range artillery piece.

situation in Khesanh "became desperate"—an idea that the Johnson administration vetoed. After the war, Westmoreland seemed to regret that nuclear weapons were not used, writing, "It could be that the use of a few small tactical nuclear weapons in Vietnam—or even the threat of them—might have quickly brought the war to an end."

U.S. and South Vietnamese forces managed to beat back enemy advances almost everywhere in the South, inflicting heavy casualties. The North Vietnamese and Vietcong lost as many as 50,000 soldiers. Some 14,000 civilians died, and more than a million new refugees were driven from their homes. And yet the Tet Offensive failed to inspire the popular uprisings that Communist leaders had predicted among the war-weary people of South Vietnam.

The fighting convinced much of the American public that the Vietnamese Communists were far from being defeated. A quick end to the war was nowhere in sight. Vietnam remained locked in the choke hold of a military stalemate that had persisted for the past three years.

In April 1968, a million students across the United States boycotted classes in a national strike against the war. President Johnson was warned that the costs of the war were damaging the American economy, threatening the president's Great Society reform programs and undermining the country's ability to maintain its military commitments elsewhere in the world.

The president called together a panel of respected foreign-policy experts, known as the Wise Men. Their advice was not encouraging.

President Johnson leans over a model of the Khesanh area in the White House Situation Room as National Security Adviser Walt Rostow points out a key battle position.

Driven from their homes during the Tet Offensive, South Vietnamese refugees trudge down a country road.

They opposed any further troop commitments. And they urged the president to stop bombing the North and to seek peace through negotiations. The time had come, the Wise Men told the president, for the United States to cut its losses and end the war.

Both sides had been calling for peace negotiations since the fighting began. Now, finally, they agreed to meet and talk in Paris. But the talks went nowhere. The North Vietnamese insisted on a total halt to the bombing before they would discuss any other subject. The United States demanded that the North pull its troops back from the South in return for a bombing halt. Neither side was willing to compromise.

As the Paris talks faltered, the fighting intensified. And 1968 became the bloodiest year of the war.

13. The Beginning of the End

President Johnson stunned the American public when he spoke to a nationwide television audience on the evening of March 31, 1968. He announced that he had ordered a halt to the bombing of North Vietnam and was ready to begin peace talks in Paris with Vietnam's Communists.

He saved the biggest surprise of his speech until the end. He had decided not to run for a second term as president. "I shall not seek, and I will not accept, the nomination of my party for another term as your president," Johnson declared.

Frustrated by the lack of progress in ending the war, and dismayed by the controversies dividing the nation, he was withdrawing as a presidential candidate in the name of "national unity," which, Johnson said, was "the ultimate strength of our country."

Despite official assurances that the war was being won, press and television coverage of the fighting and the carnage revealed a darker reality. General Westmoreland complained that biased reporting by liberal journalists had turned public opinion against the war, but if the war really was being won, then why, people asked, had Westmoreland requested 200,000 additional troops—a request that the Johnson administration rejected.

When the Paris peace talks got under way in May 1968, the fighting in Vietnam intensified. Both sides sought military gains to bolster their bargaining positions. During the course of the year, more than 14,000 American troops would be killed and 46,000 wounded despite the peace talks. The Vietnamese Communists would lose at least 200,000 killed and an unknown number wounded. In North Vietnam, army-age young men adopted a motto that they tattooed on themselves and sang songs about: "Born in the North, to die in the South." Like their American counterparts, they sought medical and educational deferments to avoid military service.

"Tomorrow . . . I go," Quang Vinh, a country boy from a village north of Hanoi, wrote in his diary as he awaited induction into the North Vietnamese army. No one in his village had ever returned from the war in the South. "Go forever, with no return. Oh, let me go and get it over with. What is the use in looking back? I am only a plain soldier. I will have only superiors."

Ten months later Vinh wrote: "Today is October 6 and we must again fight this war. We stay in the bunker all day, eat, sleep and relieve ourselves in the bunker. The enemy shelling is all around us. . . . I don't know what my fate will be. Life and death are already too close to each other. The more I think, the more I miss my father, mother, family and friends. I wish one day that I could see my family again. But that is too luxurious a wish. If I die, I only regret that I have left my country, my northern land, and could never get back to it."

Vinh's diary was found on his body by South Vietnamese paratroopers near the ruins of Quang Tai.

In the United States, antiwar demonstrations grew more violent. Protesters burned draft cards, blocked traffic and fought back as

Two children gaze at an American soldier holding a grenade launcher as they cling to their mothers huddled against a canal bank during a firefight between U.S. Marines and Vietcong guerrillas.

police tried to clear them away. The assassination of Martin Luther King Jr. on April 4 incited race riots in more than a hundred American cities. Two months later, former president Kennedy's younger brother Senator Robert F. Kennedy was shot and killed while campaigning for the presidency—adding to the foreboding sense of national crisis.

Violence reached a peak in August, when Democrats gathered in Chicago to nominate their presidential candidate for the upcoming November election. Mayor Richard Daley had mustered 12,000 police and 6,000 National Guardsmen to keep order. Outraged antiwar demonstrators, kept at a distance from the convention hall, broke through police barriers and began a march to the Hilton Hotel, where many delegates were staying. The police, provoked by taunts and pelted by sticks, stones and garbage, attacked the marchers with tear gas, eye-stinging Mace and clubs, injuring innocent bystanders. Police also assaulted reporters and photographers covering the protests, smashing their equipment. An investigative commission would describe the chaotic episode as a "police riot," marked by "unrestrained and indiscriminate police violence."

In November, Republican Richard M. Nixon was elected to succeed Lyndon Johnson as president. During the election campaign, Nixon claimed that he had a "secret plan" to end the war. Years later, he admitted that he never actually had any such plan. What he had now was a plan to win the war by means of escalation and bombing. "I'm not going to end up like LBJ," he told an aide, "holed up in the White House, afraid to show my face in the street. I'm going to stop that war. Fast. I mean it!"

Vietnam was the fly in the ointment of Nixon's efforts to

Vietcong troops pose with their new Soviet AK-47 assault rifles and captured American field radios.

normalize relations with the two big Communist powers, China and the Soviet Union. Nixon met in China with Communist Party Chairman Mao Zedong when that nation was considered a Cold War menace. He became the first U.S. president to visit the Soviet Union. But the Communists of Vietnam were harder to deal with. They would not give up their demand for a unified nation under their control. And they would not stop fighting. "We are not going to let this country be defeated by that little shit-ass country," Nixon told Henry Kissinger, his national security adviser.

Kissinger continued the peace talks in Paris with the North Vietnamese. At the same time, Nixon announced a policy of "Vietnamization," which meant building up the South Vietnamese army so that it could take on a greater share of the fighting. He began to gradually reduce the number of U.S. troops in Vietnam. But he resumed the bombing of North Vietnam, and at levels far beyond those reached by Johnson. And he authorized a secret bombing campaign against Communist bases in Cambodia, followed by a U.S.–South Vietnamese invasion of that neutral country.

None of these moves broke the military stalemate in South Vietnam. Nixon ran up against the same problems that had bedeviled his predecessors. The South Vietnamese government failed to reform itself or gain popular support. The South Vietnamese army continued to suffer from corruption, poor leadership and desertions. Even with U.S. troops at their side, and backed by American airpower, the South Vietnamese could not drive out the battered Communist forces that had been fighting to unify Vietnam for nearly twenty-five years. Despite horrendous losses, they would not give up.

As prospects for a peace settlement faded, antiwar protests surged. In October 1969, during Nixon's first year in office, 2 million Americans took part in a massive nationwide protest called the Moratorium to End the War in Vietnam. It was believed to be the largest demonstration in U.S. history. Protesters wearing black armbands to signify their dissent marched in candlelight parades. They held peaceful vigils in churches and took part in school seminars, street rallies and meetings. A second round of Moratorium protests was held a month later. By now, some 45,000 Americans had been killed in Vietnam, and almost half a million U.S. men and women were still serving there.

The American public, meanwhile, was shocked by the revelation of an unspeakable atrocity—the massacre of 504 peasants at the neighboring Vietnamese hamlets of My Lai and My Khe. Army Lieutenant William Calley had been charged with premeditated murder for his part in the massacres. Testifying before an army inquiry, Calley described brutal combat conditions in which American

Demonstrators led by Coretta Scott King hold burning candles during a night march to the White House, part of the Moratorium to End the War in Vietnam, October 15, 1969.

soldiers saw all Vietnamese as the enemy, drawing little distinction between combatants and noncombatants.

The men in Calley's company, expecting to encounter Vietcong troops or sympathizers, discovered in My Lai only a peaceful village at breakfast. Even so, they set fire to houses and attacked the unarmed villagers with gunfire and grenades. Some soldiers refused to take part in the slaughter, but that did not restrain their fellows. Most of the victims were women, children and old people. "We were all under orders," one of the riflemen recalled. "We all thought we were doing the right thing. At the time it didn't bother me."

High-ranking army officers had suppressed news of the massacres for more than a year before the story finally came out. The army filed charges ranging from murder to dereliction of duty against fourteen officers, including generals and colonels, accused of covering up the atrocity. Only one officer other than Calley ever faced a court-martial, and he was acquitted. Calley was convicted of mass murder and sentenced to life at hard labor. President Nixon intervened, ordering that Calley be released from armed custody. As a result, he served just three and a half years under house arrest.

Unidentified women and children before being killed in the My Lai massacre, March 16, 1968

News of the My Lai massacre and the secret bombing of Cambodia, when they became known, triggered a new wave of antiwar protests. At Kent State University in Ohio, demonstrating students broke windows, set fire to the building housing the Reserve Officers' Training Corps and threw stones at the

An American soldier throws a rice basket into the flames of a
burning house at My Lai.

National Guard troops called out by the governor. The guardsmen
opened fire, killing four students and wounding nine others. Two of
the dead students were not even part of the protest, but were shot
while crossing the campus on their way to class.

More unsettling revelations surfaced in 1971, when the *New
York Times* published excerpts of a top secret U.S. government study
known as the Pentagon Papers. The mammoth stack of papers—some
7,000 pages—documented the history of the American involvement
in Vietnam and confirmed many of the suspicions held by the war's
opponents. Included was the cable confirming U.S. participation in
the coup that toppled South Vietnamese president Diem and the
secret intelligence assessments stating that the war could not be
won at any reasonable cost. President Nixon asked the U.S. Supreme
Court to ban further publication of the papers. The court denied

Mary Ann Vecchio kneels over the body of twenty-year-old student Jeffrey Miller, shot by Ohio National Guard troops during an antiwar demonstration at Kent State University, May 4, 1970.

his appeal in a landmark decision upholding freedom of the press.

According to a 1971 poll, 58 percent of Americans believed that the war in Vietnam was "morally wrong" and 60 percent favored the withdrawal of U.S. troops, even if it meant the collapse of the South Vietnamese government.

Mounting antiwar sentiment at home spread to GIs in the field. "In a month of visiting units in the field and rear areas around Military Region One," wrote *New York Times* reporter Donald Kirk, "I found literally no GIs in favor of the war, none who didn't think we should 'get out.'"

As President Nixon continued to withdraw troops, the war seemed to be drawing down. "Once we've decided to get out, and then keep fighting, it seems kind of worthless," a young officer told Kirk. "Nobody wants to be the last guy to die in Vietnam."

Doubts about the goals and morality of the war led to a breakdown in military discipline and morale. Soldiers began to question why they were in Vietnam. Many of the men wore peace symbols on their helmets and uniforms. Some balked at going into combat. Racial tensions surfaced in once-cordial units when blacks and whites no longer shared a sense of purpose. A new word entered the language as officers and NCOs were wounded or killed by exploding grenades in "fragging" attacks carried out by their own troops.

As morale sagged, drug use became widespread. A Department of Defense survey found that half the GIs in Vietnam were smoking marijuana and a quarter or more used opium or its derivative, heroin.

In 1971, the *Armed Forces Journal* reported, "The morale, discipline and battle-worthiness of the U.S. armed forces are, with a few

A peace symbol flies atop an armored vehicle at an American military outpost near the border of Laos.

Members of the 1st Calvary Division carry a wounded comrade to safety while under heavy shelling from North Vietnamese troops.

salient exceptions, lower and worse than at any time in this century and possibly in the history of the United States."

Contrary to some movies about the Vietnam War, most of the drug and discipline problems were in the rear-echelon bases—not on the front lines. The combat units largely remained effective. "Most men here believe that we will *not* win the war," one soldier said. "And yet they stick their necks out every day."

American GIs—the faithful "grunts" who bore the brunt of the fighting—continued valiantly to put their lives on the line in service of a war in which many no longer believed. One of the men in Philip Caputo's infantry company strayed into a minefield: "He was blasted into the air, and his left foot turned into a mass of bruised and bloody meat inside the tatters of his boot. He might have bled to death out there, but Lance Corporal Sampson, crawling on his belly and probing for mines with a bayonet, cleared a path through the field, slung the wounded man over his shoulder, and carried him to safety."

Sampson was recommended for a Bronze Star. The wounded rifleman was evacuated to the States, where his foot was amputated.

"They were all Marines, and they took care of each other," a navy chaplain recalled. "They would dash out in the middle of incoming [fire] and drag a total stranger who had been hit. It goes beyond camaraderie. It's like they were a single organism. Theologically, I can use the term 'love'—they really loved each other, by how they lived and what they did."

14. The Fall of Saigon

In January 1972, President Nixon revealed that Kissinger had been holding secret talks with the North Vietnamese for the past two years. When the talks stalled, the Communists launched another major offensive, known in the West as the Easter Offensive.

On March 30, 120,000 North Vietnamese troops, equipped with Soviet-made tanks and artillery, struck at targets throughout South Vietnam, scoring quick victories. At the time, only 95,000 U.S. personnel remained in Vietnam, including just 6,000 combat-ready troops. The defense burden lay mainly with the South Vietnamese army.

Nixon, facing a reelection campaign in November, was concerned that the North's onslaught would topple the Saigon regime and result in a humiliating American defeat. He responded to the new offensive by ordering round-the-clock bombing of North Vietnam—the first such attacks in more than three years—and against advancing enemy troops in the South. "The bastards have never been bombed like they're going to be bombed this time," he vowed.

Nixon's goal was to pull the remaining U.S. forces out of Vietnam while avoiding any appearance of an American defeat—to achieve what he called "peace with honor." Anything less, he believed, would destroy America's credibility as a world power. Like Lyndon Johnson before him, Richard Nixon did not want to be the first American president to lose a war.

A South Vietnamese soldier with antitank rockets at his side during the Easter Offensive in the spring of 1972

The North Vietnamese returned to the negotiating table in July, and this time both sides were willing to make concessions. By early fall, a tentative agreement was in sight. On October 26, Kissinger announced, "Peace is at hand." Twelve days later, President Nixon won a landslide victory in his bid for reelection. But Kissinger's optimism was premature. The talks broke down again over the status of the South Vietnamese government and its current president, Nguyen Van Thieu.

Nixon ordered another aerial onslaught. During eleven days in December, dubbed the Christmas Bombing by the American press, B-52s dropped more bombs on North Vietnam, mostly on Hanoi and Haiphong, than the total tonnage unleashed during the previous three years. On December 26, the North suffered the most intense day of aerial bombardment in world history. The next day, the North Vietnamese government announced that it was ready to reopen negotiations as soon as the bombing stopped.

Four weeks later, on January 23, 1973, the United States, North Vietnam, South Vietnam and the Vietcong signed the Paris Peace Agreement, which preserved, for the time being, an independent South Vietnam. The pact provided for the withdrawal of all remaining U.S. troops, the return of U.S. prisoners of war, and a cease-fire between the opposing Vietnamese forces. The fighting stopped, but not for long.

The last U.S. combat troops left Vietnam on March 29, 1973. Only a small detachment of marines stayed behind, to guard the U.S. embassy in Saigon. On April 1, North Vietnam released the 591 U.S. prisoners of war it had been holding, some for as long as eight years, under harsh and sometimes brutal conditions. Because the U.S. had never officially declared war against Vietnam, the North Vietnamese had refused to give American POWs the rights required by international law. Some prisoners were tortured during interrogations to extract military information.

"There was a sense of unity, togetherness, shared adversity," said Gerald Coffee, a navy aviator who was imprisoned for seven years and was among the first group to be released. "We came home and our release kind of symbolized the end of a very painful chapter in our nation's history."

North Vietnamese POWs captured in the South were also released after the peace agreement. They had been routinely beaten, tortured and, at times, executed during the undeclared war.

President Nixon declared that he had achieved the "peace with honor" he had promised. But Henry Kissinger acknowledged that, at best, the peace agreement provided for a "decent interval" between the American withdrawal and the ultimate fate of South Vietnam.

The American troops went home. Soldiers returning from earlier wars had been greeted as conquering heroes. This time there were no national parades or celebrations to welcome home Vietnam veterans. They were embraced by their families but met by the public with stony silence. Many veterans who had been wounded would suffer lifelong disabilities. Many others, returning with painful memories, were afflicted with a persistent condition called posttraumatic stress disorder, trigged by experiencing or witnessing a terrible event.

The United States continued to maintain a commanding presence of advisers, officials and intelligence agents in Saigon. Huge amounts of American military and economic aid still propped up the South Vietnamese government. And U.S. bombers continued to pound Communist sanctuaries in Cambodia until Congress demanded an end to *all* military operations in Indochina.

The peace accord called for a National Council of Reconciliation, composed of factions from both North and South Vietnam, including the existing Saigon government under President Thieu, the Communist-dominated Provisional Revolutionary Government and a coalition of neutralist parties. This council was to supervise national elections that would determine the nation's future. But the

Recently released American POWs, mostly aviators captured when their planes were shot down, being flown from Hanoi to Clark Air Force Base in the Philippines aboard the affectionately named "Hanoi Taxi," March 1973

Released prisoner of war Lt. Colonel Robert L. Stirm is greeted
by his family as he returns home from the Vietnam War.

settlement broke down almost immediately. Neither Saigon nor
Hanoi was willing to compromise on the election plans. Both sides
violated the cease-fire. By 1974 a full-scale war was raging again
as Vietcong and North Vietnamese forces fought to overthrow the
Saigon regime.

The Nixon presidency, meanwhile, was about to unravel. Threat-
ened with impeachment for his role in the cover-up of political es-
pionage and "dirty tricks" known as the Watergate scandal, Nixon
resigned in disgrace on August 9, 1974. He was replaced by Vice President Gerald Ford. By then an overwhelming majority of Americans
wanted to end all U.S. involvement in Vietnam.

Without the backing of American troops, the South Vietnamese
army proved no match for the Vietcong guerrillas and North Vietnam
regulars. Communist troops swept through the South, capturing one
city after another, sometimes without a battle. President Ford saw

no hope of rescuing the Saigon regime. When Ford's military advisers urged him to resume the air war, the president replied, "I can't. The country is fed up with the war."

As North Vietnamese troops and tanks closed in on Saigon, President Thieu fled the country, declaring bitterly that America had betrayed him. A week later, on April 29, 1975, the United States began a desperate and chaotic evacuation of American personnel in Saigon, along with South Vietnamese who had worked closely with the United States. Those left behind would face harsh retribution as collaborators.

Like the war itself, the exit from Vietnam raised difficult moral questions. Who among the vulnerable Vietnamese would be evacuated, and who would be left behind? Over a span of eighteen hours, a fleet of seventy marine helicopters lifted thousands of Americans and Vietnamese to ships waiting offshore. U.S. Marines struggled to control mobs of desperate people surging toward the helicopter takeoff pads, attempting to climb aboard.

Carrying their belongings, evacuees cross the deck of a navy ship waiting to take them to the Philippines. Most of them will be resettled in the United States.

A helicopter packed with South Vietnamese evacuees lands on the deck of the aircraft carrier USS *Midway,* April 29, 1975.

Vietnamese trying to get out of the country surrounded the U.S. embassy. "They were screaming, crying, trampling one another, and some clawed at the gates in their futile effort to get inside the embassy compound," reported Bob Tamarkin of the *Chicago Daily News.* Helicopters hovered overhead with their red lights blinking, landed in the embassy courtyard or on the roof and then, jammed with passengers, lifted off and headed for the waiting ships in the China Sea.

"The scene at the embassy wall was brutal," Tamarkin wrote. The barbed wire atop the wall had been pushed aside at one point, yet people still became tangled in it as they tried to climb over. "The marines began pulling people up. In some cases, families were separated forever. They were hoisted up and over like sacks of potatoes, dumped wherever they landed."

In one dramatic episode, a Vietnamese pilot flew his family in a Chinook helicopter to the USS *Kirk.* The helicopter was too big to land on the small ship, so it hovered overhead as the pilot's family jumped one after another down to the deck. A baby was tossed and caught below. The pilot then hovered over the water, jumped, and swam to the ship.

Reporter Tamarkin was aboard one of the last helicopters to leave Saigon. "The passengers, including me, sat stoically in the dark, tired and numb. Some were dazed, finding it difficult to believe that the Americans were pulling out in this manner, skulking away in the darkness." Hundreds of Vietnamese were left behind in the embassy compound, along with thousands of others throughout the country who had been promised evacuation.

The long road to revolution ended at the entrance to the presidential palace in the heart of Saigon. On the morning of April 30, 1975, a North Vietnamese tank smashed through the palace gates and rolled into the spacious courtyard. One of the crew jumped out, ran up the palace stairs, unfurled the Vietcong flag and hung it from a balcony.

A burst of gunfire followed. A small group of South Vietnamese officials were waiting in a reception room, prepared to surrender to Colonel Bui Tin, the ranking North Vietnamese officer. When they heard the rifle fire, they ducked. "Our men are merely celebrating," the colonel told them. "You have nothing to fear. Between Vietnamese, there are no victors and no vanquished. Only the

Last stop on the road to revolution: A North Vietnamese tank enters the gates of the presidential palace in Saigon, April 30, 1975.

A Vietnamese farmer carries his grown son, a victim of birth defects associated with the spraying of Agent Orange.

Americans have been beaten. If you are patriots, consider this a moment of joy. The war for our country is over."

Vietnam was now united, independent and Communist. During thirty years of war, as many as 3 million Vietnamese soldiers and civilians had been killed—no one knows exactly how many. An equal number had been maimed or crippled by bombings, shellings and land mines, or suffered birth defects and illnesses caused by the use of Agent Orange.

In Washington, D.C., the names of more than 58,000 American soldiers who died in a war that was never officially declared are inscribed on the Vietnam Veterans Memorial wall. It is one of the capital's most heavily visited sites.

The last American soldier to die in the Vietnam War was Private First Class Kelton Rena Turner, an eighteen-year-old African-American marine. He was killed in action two weeks after the evacuation of Saigon during a battle to rescue the crew of the *Mayaguez*, a merchant ship hijacked off the coast of Cambodia by the Communist Khmer Rouge. Forty other soldiers also lost their lives during the fourteen-hour firefight known as the Mayaguez Incident, regarded as the last battle of the war. Because of a failure in communications, the soldiers who fought and died that day were not aware that the crew members they were trying to save had already been set free by the Communists.

15. Reconciliation

Following their victory, the Communists changed the name of Saigon to Ho Chi Minh City, but locals continued to call it Saigon. Today a large statue of Ho, seated and holding a child, stands in a park outside City Hall. If statues could see, Ho would be looking at a luxury hotel on one side, a Brooks Brothers store in an opulent French colonial building on the other, and all around a neighborhood filled with fashionable shops, popular restaurants and cafés, and a frenzy of buying and selling that the *New York Times* described as "voraciously capitalistic."

Four decades after the war ended, Vietnam was a country at peace, with a flourishing free-market economy. The name cards of government officials still said Socialist Republic of Vietnam, but the bustling streets told a different story. "If, for Americans, the war . . . was on some level about keeping Vietnam safe for capitalism, it turns out that they need not have worried," the *Times* reported. "Capitalism here churns relentlessly, aided by what Ted Osius, the United States ambassador, has called 'the most entrepreneurial people on earth.'"

In 1975, when the Communists took power, they imposed an

A statue of Ho Chi Minh outside City Hall in Ho Chi Minh City

uncompromising political rule on the country. Hundreds of thousands of suspected political foes were arrested and sent to harsh "reeducation" camps, some for many years. One of the worst camps was Poulo Condore, the island where the French jailed Communist suspects during the 1930s and where the South Vietnamese regime imprisoned its critics during the 1950s and 1960s. The Communists were no kinder to their prisoners than their oppressors had been to them. Inmates died of malnutrition, overwork, disease and neglect. Thousands were tortured or executed.

Faced with catastrophic war damage, the Communists also imposed a rigid socialist economy. They abolished private commerce and pursued disastrous experiments with collectivized farms, causing critical food shortages and a near famine. Hundreds of thousands of embittered refugees—no one knows exactly how many—fled the country between 1975 and 1995, often in small, rickety boats.

Buffeted by storms, attacked by pirates, turned away from foreign ports, many of these "boat people" perished before they could find new homes. More than half the boat people were resettled in the United States, and most of the others in France, Canada, Australia and Great Britain.

"Yes, we defeated the United States," said Vietnamese Prime Minister Pham Van Dong. "But now we are plagued with problems. We do not have enough to eat. We are a poor, undeveloped nation. Waging a war is simple, but running a country is very difficult."

In 1989, the year the Berlin Wall came down and the Soviet Union collapsed, Vietnam's leaders abruptly changed course. They reversed the farm collectivization program and began to introduce a market economy. Along with a growing acceptance of free enterprise, they

Vietnamese boat people wait to be rescued by the USS *Blue Ridge* after spending eight days at sea in a thirty-five-foot fishing boat, May 15, 1984.

Rush hour in Ho Chi Minh City, aka Saigon, March 2011

expanded civil liberties, though the Communist Party kept its monopoly on power. In 2015, state-owned companies made up about one-quarter of the economy, but private and foreign enterprises were what kept the economy growing.

A historic meeting in the summer of 2015 revealed just how much times had changed. President Barack Obama warmly welcomed the head of Vietnam's Communist Party to the White House and spoke of visiting that country in the future. The meeting was timed to mark the twentieth anniversary of normalized relations between the one-time enemies. Obama declared that the United States and Vietnam had moved beyond their "difficult history" and would continue to cooperate on trade and regional security issues.

Sitting beside Nguyen Phu Trong, the Communist Party boss, in the Oval Office, the president praised "the remarkable progress that's taken place in the relationship between our two countries over the last twenty years. I certainly look forward to visiting your beautiful country sometime in the future."

The two leaders had a frank discussion about human-rights abuses by Vietnam's one-party Communist government. "We discussed candidly our differences around human rights, for example, and freedom of religion," the president said. "But what I'm confident about is that the diplomatic dialogue and practical steps we are taking will benefit both countries, that these tensions can be resolved in an effective fashion."

And so the dreaded consequence of falling dominoes, which had haunted American foreign policy, never came to pass. Communist takeovers in Vietnam and its neighbors, Cambodia and Laos, did not topple the other nations of the region. Communist forces never menaced "the beaches of Waikiki," as President Johnson had warned. The falling-domino theory proved in the end to be a mirage.

President Barack Obama greets Communist Party General Secretary
Nguyen Phu Trong in the Oval Office of the White House, July 7, 2015.

Americans have disagreed bitterly on why the United States lost the war. Some blame biased media coverage and the antiwar movement for undermining the war effort. They argue that a succession of timid civilian leaders did not permit the military to do what was necessary to win, which meant sending more troops and intensifying the bombing. Instead, they say, American soldiers were forced to fight "with one hand tied behind their backs."

An opposite point of view contends that the war could not have been "won" at an acceptable cost of lives and dollars, that America's vast technological superiority could not prevail over the tenacity of a determined foe. After the war, the Vietminh's General Giap was asked how long he would have gone on fighting against the United States. "Another twenty years, maybe a hundred years, as long as it took to win, regardless of the cost," he replied.

The Vietnamese Communists saw the struggle as a total war for the survival of themselves and their cause, another chapter in their country's resistance to foreign rule. For the United States, Vietnam was a limited war, one battle among others as part of the ongoing Cold War.

"First, we didn't know ourselves," General Maxwell Taylor told war correspondent and historian Stanley Karnow. "We thought we were going into another Korean War, but this was a different country. Second, we didn't know our South Vietnamese allies. We never understood them. That was another surprise. And we knew even less about North Vietnam. . . . So, until we know the enemy and know our allies and know ourselves, we'd better keep out of this kind of dirty business. It's very dangerous."

In other words, the United States should have pursued, as some commentators suggested, a *political* rather than a *military* solution.

The American defeat was caused by a failure to understand the history, culture and needs of the Vietnamese people, who thought they were fighting for independence and the right to determine their own destiny.

Front cover of *The Word: Ho Chi Minh City*, "The What's On Guide to Vietnam," an English-language publication

George Ball, a senior State Department official in the Kennedy and Johnson administrations, argued against American involvement in Vietnam. Looking back, he called the war "probably the greatest single error made by America in its history." Robert McNamara, secretary of defense under Kennedy and Johnson, supported American intervention to begin with, but changed his mind as he came to recognize the war's futility. "We were wrong, terribly wrong," he concluded in his anguished memoir. "We owe it to future generations to explain why."

Can nations learn from their wars? Immediately after the war, the United States and Vietnam regarded each other warily, with suspicion and mistrust. Over the years, the two countries overcame a number of difficult issues and established a friendship forged by the interaction of their peoples. Growing numbers of American tourists, investors and veterans visit Vietnam every year. Some veterans have moved to Vietnam to live and work among the people they once regarded as enemies. They are often surprised by how warmly they are welcomed.

In a poll published in 2015, 78 percent of Vietnamese said they had a favorable impression of the United States. Among those under thirty years old, it was 88 percent.

"I've learned how to forgive from the Vietnamese," said Chuck

An American marine pays his respects at the Vietnam Veterans Memorial.

Palazzo, a retired marine and the owner of a software company in Danang. "I've learned from them to keep looking forward."

Some Vietnamese who fled to the United States after the war have returned home to start businesses. In 2014, more than 16,000 Vietnamese students were enrolled at American universities. And an increasing number of Vietnam's diplomats and business leaders were educated in the United States.

Peter Peterson served as the first U.S. ambassador to Vietnam when diplomatic relations were reestablished in 1995. A former Air Force pilot, he was shot down over Hanoi and spent six and a half years as a prisoner of war. When Peterson returned to Hanoi on a visit, a reporter asked him why the United States and Vietnam, friends today, had to fight such a long and destructive war. "I have thought about this for a long time," Peterson said. "I'm convinced that the war could have been averted had we made the effort to understand the politics of the place."

The United States emerged from World War II as the mightiest superpower on earth, a beacon of liberty and a model for countries everywhere. Vietnam shook Americans' faith in the wisdom of their leaders and the moral authority of their country. In the future, they would more readily question authority. The Vietnam War was also a humbling reminder of the limits of power. And as time passed and enemies reconciled, it was a lesson in the power of forgiveness.

In August 2015, a month after President Obama's White House meeting with Communist Party leader Nguyen Phu Trong, John Kerry returned to Vietnam, where he had served as a U.S. Navy lieutenant during the 1960s. Meeting with Communist Party leaders in Hanoi, Kerry, now America's top diplomat as Obama's secretary of state, hailed Vietnam's transformation from enemy to friend. "In twenty years [since diplomatic ties were established] we have traveled a remarkable distance," Kerry said. "The journey of reconciliation between our countries is really one of the great stories of nations that once were at war being able to find common ground and create a new relationship."

When CBS television reporter Morley Safer returned to Vietnam in 1989, a former Vietcong guerrilla handed him the following poem, written in honor of returning GIs:

> *How many American soldiers*
> *Died in this land?*
> *How many Vietnamese*
> *Lie buried under trees and grass . . .*
> *Now the wineglass joins friends in peace.*
> *The old men lift their glasses.*
> *Tears run down their cheeks.*

TIME LINE

1859   French troops capture Saigon.

1883   France divides Vietnam into three parts, establishing "protectorates" over Annam and Tonkin, and ruling Cochinchina as a French colony.

1890   Ho Chi Minh is born in a Vietnamese village, May 19.

1911   Ho leaves Vietnam as a crew member on a French freighter. He will not return for thirty years.

1919   Ho and his fellow exiles present a petition to the Paris Peace Conference, asking self-determination for Vietnam. The petition is ignored.

1920   Ho joins the newly formed French Communist Party.

1930   Meeting secretly in Hong Kong, Ho and his fellow exiles form the Indochinese Communist Party.

        French suppress anti-colonial uprisings throughout Vietnam, imprisoning thousands of suspected Communists and executing 2,000.

1940   As World War II begins, Japan occupies Vietnam but leaves the French colonial administration in charge of the government.

1941   Ho returns secretly to Vietnam and forms the Vietminh to fight both the Japanese and the French.

1945   Ho meets with American intelligence agents at a guerrilla camp near Hanoi to arrange mutual assistance.

        Japan surrenders to the Allies, August 15.

        Ho proclaims the independence of Vietnam, September 2.

1946   French forces seize control of Vietnamese cities, expelling the Communist Vietminh and beginning the French war in Vietnam.

1954   The French are defeated at the Battle of Dienbienphu, May 7.

        The Geneva Conference divides Vietnam in half pending nationwide elections to unify the country.

A captured American warplane on display outside the War Remnants Museum in Ho Chi Minh City

1955   Backed by the U.S., Ngo Dinh Diem rejects the Geneva Accords, refuses to take part in nationwide elections and proclaims himself president of the Republic of Vietnam.

1957   President Dwight D. Eisenhower reaffirms U.S. support for the Diem regime.

Communist insurgency begins in South Vietnam.

1960   Communist leaders in Hanoi form the National Liberation Front for South Vietnam, also known as the Vietcong.

1961   Newly elected President John F. Kennedy expands economic and military aid to South Vietnam, increasing the number of military advisers from 200 to 12,000.

1963   Diem is overthrown in a coup led by rebel generals supported by the U.S., November 1.

Kennedy is assassinated in Dallas, Texas, November 22.

1964   General Nguyen Khanh seizes power in Saigon, January 30. Khanh will be followed by a succession of weak and unpopular governments.

South Vietnamese torpedo boats begin secret raids against North Vietnamese coastal installations in July.

North Vietnamese patrol boats attack U.S. destroyer in the Tonkin Gulf, August 2. President Lyndon B. Johnson orders first U.S. air strikes against North Vietnam.

Congress passes Tonkin Gulf Resolution, August 7.

1965   Operation Rolling Thunder, the sustained bombing of North Vietnam, begins on February 24.

The first U.S. combat troops arrive in Vietnam, March 8.

American troop strength in Vietnam reaches 200,000 by year's end.

1966   American troop strength reaches nearly 400,000.

1967   Defense Secretary Robert McNamara testifies that bombing of North Vietnam is having little effect.

American troop strength reaches 500,000.

1968   Tet Offensive begins as Vietcong and North Vietnamese forces launch attacks throughout South Vietnam, January 31.

Johnson orders bombing halt, agrees to peace talks, and says he will not run for reelection, March 31.

Martin Luther King Jr. is assassinated in Memphis, April 4.

Senator Robert F. Kennedy is assassinated in Los Angeles, June 5.

Richard M. Nixon is elected president of the United States, November 5.

American troop strength in Vietnam reaches 540,000.

1969   Nixon begins secret bombing of neutral Cambodia, March 18.

Ho Chi Minh dies in Hanoi at age seventy-nine, September 2.

Two million Americans join in Moratorium to End the War in Vietnam on October 15 and again on November 15.

The My Lai massacre, which took place in March 1968, is revealed twenty months later on November 16, 1969.

1970   Henry Kissinger begins secret peace talks in Paris with North Vietnamese, February 20.

Ohio National Guardsmen kill four students at Kent State University during antiwar demonstration, May 4.

American troop strength in Vietnam is reduced to 280,000 under Nixon's Vietnamization policy.

1971   Lieutenant William Calley is convicted of mass murder at My Lai, March 29.

The *New York Times* begins publication of the Pentagon Papers, June 13.

American troop strength in Vietnam is reduced to 140,000 by December.

1972   North Vietnam launches Easter Offensive, March 30.
Nixon orders resumption of round-the-clock bombing of North Vietnam, April 15.

Nixon is reelected, November 7.

With Paris peace talks stalled, Nixon orders intensified bombing raids around Hanoi and Haiphong, December 18.

1973   Paris peace talks resume on January 8. Agreement is reached on January 23.

Last American troops leave Vietnam, March 29.

In July, Congress demands an end to military operations in Indochina, and on August 14, the United States stops the secret bombing of Cambodia.

1974   As the peace accords break down, war begins again between North and South Vietnam.

Faced with impeachment, Nixon resigns on August 9 and is replaced by his vice president, Gerald Ford.

1975   Communist troops sweep through South Vietnam, capturing Hue on March 25 and Danang on March 30.

South Vietnam's President Thieu flees Saigon, April 25.

Evacuation of Americans from Saigon begins, April 29.

Communist forces capture Saigon, April 30.

1977   President Jimmy Carter, on his first day in office, pardons all Vietnam War draft evaders, January 21.

1995   The United States and Vietnam establish full diplomatic relations, July 11.

SOURCE NOTES

Chapter One

Page

2   ENOUGH . . . OUT NOW: James M. Naughton, "200,000 Rally in Capital to End War," *New York Times*, April 25, 1971

3–4   "corrupt and dictatorial . . . for a mistake?": Vietnam Veterans Against the War statement by John Kerry to Senate Committee on Foreign Relations, April 23, 1971 (http://www2.iath.virginia.edu/sixties/HTML_docs/Resources/Primary/Manifestos/VVAW_Kerry_Senate.html)

4   "noble cause": Lawrence, p. 175

Chapter Two

6   "Although we have . . . lacked heroes": Becker, p. 3

7–8   "We have had . . . disappear into nowhere": Lockard, p. 104

8   "The rich to give . . . the invader": Karnow, p. 120

9   "Let us, gentlemen . . . a possession": Langer, p. 4

9   "Paris of the Orient": Fitzgerald, p. 55

11   "Oh, the old days . . . too high": Trullinger, p. 18

12   "backward country": Fitzgerald, p. 212

12   "civilize inferior peoples": Karnow, p. 96

12   "The Vietnamese . . . second place": Fitzgerald, p. 296

Chapter Three

13   "he seemed . . . mocking himself": Karnow, p. 109

14   "It was patriotism . . . inspired me": Ibid., p. 134

Chapter Four

19   "a pile of bones . . . yellow skin": Ibid., p. 150

21   "politics. . . . the country": Dommen, p. 97

21   "The Vietnamese . . . couple of times": Karnow, p. 150

Inside the War Remnants Museum, Vietnamese schoolgirls consider the horrors of a war that took place before they were born.

Page

21–22   "Giap wanted . . . blown off": Douglas Martin, "Henry A. Prunier, 91, U.S. Soldier Who Trained Vietnamese Troops, Dies, *New York Times,* April 24, 2013, p. A17

22   "The decisive hour . . . free ourselves": Ho Chi Minh, p. 50

24   "The Vietnam War . . . first place": Interview with Archimedes L. A. Patti, 1981 (http://openvault.wgbh.org/catalog/vietnam-bf3262-interview-with-archimedes-1-a-patti-1981)

24   "Ho saw . . . he was naïve": Martin, *New York Times,* April 24, 2013

25–26   "All men . . . happy and free": Ho Chi Minh, p. 53

26   "If we departed . . . start again": Asprey, p. 477

26–27   "Don't you realize . . . finished in Asia": Ruane, p. 14

28   "All Vietnamese . . . hoes or sticks": Ho Chi Minh, p. 68

Chapter Five

30   "to support . . . re-conquer Indochina": Arendt, p. 29

30–31   "We apparently . . . on ourselves": Sheehan, p. 149

32   "No one here . . . behind him": Trullinger, p. 59

32   "If those gooks . . . they'll get it": Karnow, p. 172

32   "a severe lesson": Sheehan, p. 149

33   "If the tiger . . . bleed to death": Ruane, p. 19

Page

60 "Let them burn . . . clap our hands": Joseph R. Gregory, "Madame Nhu, Vietnam War Lightning Rod, Dies," *New York Times,* April 27, 2011, p. B16

60 "Saigon . . . able to do": Fitzgerald, p. 75

61 "My God! . . . coming apart": Jones, p. 319

61 "We are launched . . . Diem administration": Sheehan, p. 360

61 "the Viet Cong . . . in the war": Ibid., p. 364

61 "I am ready . . . leave the country": Karnow, p. 324

62–63 "For the sake . . . foreign affairs": *Reporting Vietnam,* p. 48

Chapter Nine

64 "The prospects . . . shorter war": Karnow, p. 327

64–66 "my best guess . . . we realized": Sheehan, p. 376

66 "ineffective . . . each other": Karnow, p. 363

67 "If I . . . an appeaser": *Reporting Vietnam,* p. 475

67–68 "terrible . . . worse than that": Dallek, *Lyndon B. Johnson,* p. 220

68 "to seek . . . I took": Ruane, p. 64

68 "open aggression on the high seas": Ibid., p. 64

69 "Our national . . . defending it": Alterman, p. 198

69 "I believe . . . historic mistake": Halberstam, p. 419

70 "economical with the truth": Ruane, p. 65

70 "We are not . . . for themselves": Lawrence, p. 87

71 "mounting feeling . . . guerrilla war": Becker, p. 93

71–72 "We are playing . . . get out": Associated Press, "LBJ Viewed Vietnam in '64 as 'Damn Mess,' Tapes Show," *Los Angeles Times,* February 15, 1997

73 "makes the chills . . . my back": Ruane, p. 67

73 "concentrate on finding . . . out of control": Karnow, p. 343

73 "pouring . . . wrong place": Arendt, p. 27

Chapter Ten

74 "America seemed . . . we lost": Caputo, p. xiv

76 "We were going . . . enterprise": Ibid., p. 69

77 "Call the Shelter . . . Home": Duiker, *Sacred War,* p. 200

77 "Our home . . . blood and bone" : Ibid

Page

77   "not to conquer . . . South Vietnam": Langer, p. 295

78   "The Americans . . . our spirit": Karnow, p. 473

78   "Enemy operations . . . its people": McNamara, *Argument Without End,* p. 252

79   "The napalm . . . months later": Karnow, p. 473

80–81   "You go out . . . with him": Appy, pp. 163–64

81–82   "You never knew . . . around you": MacKenzie, p. 110

82–83   "A phosphorous grenade . . . paying the price": Caputo, pp. 109–110

83   "If [the villagers] . . . we left": Tirman, p. 154

83–84   "The thought . . . the French": Karnow, p. 174

84   "This being . . . for them": *Reporting Vietnam*:, pp. 194–198

Chapter Eleven

85   "It was a time . . . people took": Jeff Leen, "The Vietnam Protests: When Worlds Collided," *Washington Post,* September 27, 1999, p. A1

86   "The Great Society . . . battlefields of Vietnam": Karnow, p. 488

86–87   "The suffering poor . . . in Vietnam": Martin Luther King Jr., "Declaration of Independence from the War in Vietnam" (http://www.salsa.net/peace/conv/8weekconv4-3.html)

88   "The great majority . . . production lines": *Reporting Vietnam,* p. 465

88   NO MORE . . . PEACE NOW: Leen, *Washington Post,* September 27, 1999

89   "Will you . . . flowers?": Ibid.

90   "We are . . . our pressures": Schmitz, pp. 54–56

91   "We have reached . . . into view": James H. Willbanks, "Winning the Battle, Losing the War," *New York Times,* March 5, 2008

91   "The picture . . . pretty one": McNamara, *In Retrospect,* p. 269

Chapter Twelve

94   "My first . . . weird music": Karnow, p. 545

94–95   "There had been . . . wispy, delicate, dead": Herr, p. 84

96   "Communists . . . barbed wire": Caputo, pp. xviii–xix

96   "at all costs": Kaku, p. 159

97   "It could be . . . an end": Ibid., p. 159

Chapter Thirteen

Page

100   "I shall not . . . our country": Tom Wicker, "Johnson Says He Won't Run," *New York Times,* April 1, 1968, p. 1

101   "Born in the North, to die in the South": Spector, p. 82

101   "Tomorrow . . . back to it": *Reporting Vietnam,* pp. 656–58

103   "police riot . . . police violence": Walker Report summary at History of the Federal Judiciary, The Chicago Seven Conspiracy Trial (http://www.fjc.gov/history/home.nsf/page/tu_chicago7_doc_13.html)

103   "I'm not . . . I mean it!": Haldeman, p. 120

104   "We are not . . . country": Dallek, p. 372

106   "We were . . . bother me": Seymour M. Hersh, "The Scene of the Crime," *The New Yorker*, March 30, 2015, p. 54

108   "morally wrong": Lawrence, p. 151

108   "In a month . . . 'get out.'": *Reporting Vietnam*, p. 524

108–109   "Once we've decided . . . die in Vietnam": Ibid., p. 538

109–110   "The morale . . . the United States": Hunt, p. 122

110   "Most men . . . every day": Becker, p. 143

110–111   "He was blasted . . . to safety": Caputo, p. 63

111   "They were . . . what they did": "A Decade in the War That Changed Everything," *AARP The Magazine*, April/May 2015, p. 59

Chapter Fourteen

112   "The bastards . . . this time": Reeves, p. 466

113   "peace with honor": Ruane, p. 90

113   "Peace is at hand": Lawrence, p. 158

114   "There was a sense . . . nation's history": Wyatt Olson, "40 Years After Release, POWs at Hanoi Hilton Reflect on Experience," *Stars and Stripes,* February 10, 2013

114   "decent interval": Lawrence, p. 152

117   "I can't . . . the war": Duiker, *Sacred War,* p. 246

118   "They were screaming . . . compound": *Reporting Vietnam,* p. 749

118   "The scene . . . landed": Ibid., pp. 748–49

GLOSSARY

AGENT ORANGE A toxic chemical, sprayed from aircraft and riverboats, used by U.S. forces to poison crops and destroy the jungle cover, depriving the enemy of food and hiding places. Agent Orange was later found to cause cancer, birth defects and other serious illnesses among U.S. servicemen and their families and Vietnamese peasants exposed to the chemical.

ATTRITION STRATEGY General William Westmoreland's plan to wear down the Communist insurgency by inflicting such heavy casualties, measured by the daily body count, that the enemy would lose the will and ability to continue the war.

BOAT PEOPLE Political and economic refugees who fled from Communist Vietnam, often in small overcrowded boats, between 1975 and 1995. Thousands drowned. Most were resettled in the United States and other countries.

COLD WAR The dangerous military rivalry between the United States and the Soviet Union, both nuclear powers, that began at the end of World War II in 1945 and lasted until the early 1990s.

CONTAINMENT The U.S. policy adopted by President Harry Truman to contain Soviet Communism where it already existed and prevent it from spreading elsewhere.

DOMINO THEORY A term coined by President Dwight D. Eisenhower, suggesting that if Vietnam fell to the Communists, then other nations nearby would topple as well, tumbling one after another like a row of falling dominoes. The theory was eventually discredited.

FRAGGING A word coined by disaffected troops in Vietnam to describe attacks with exploding fragmentation grenades and booby traps that injured and sometimes killed unpopular officers and NCOs.

FREE-FIRE ZONE An area open to unrestricted artillery and mortar fire and strafing from helicopter gunships, where anything that moves can be killed and anything standing can be leveled.

NAPALM A jelly-like substance that burns whatever it touches—trees, buildings and people.

NATIONAL LIBERATION FRONT OF SOUTH VIETNAM A broad-based coalition of political groups, organized by the leaders of North Vietnam, to work toward the unification of Vietnam and the removal of American military forces. The NLF directed a guerrilla insurgency in the South popularly known as the Vietcong—an abbreviation of the words for Vietnamese Communists.

SEARCH AND DESTROY OPERATIONS U.S. military operations that sought to locate and annihilate enemy troop concentrations. Search and destroy operations inflicted heavy civilian casualties as infantry troops swept through villages probing for enemy hiding places.

STRATEGIC HAMLETS Fortified villages, often miles from ancestral villages, set up by the South Vietnam army and its American advisers to isolate peasants from Vietcong insurgents. Millions of peasants were moved, sometimes forcibly, to the hamlets, which were eventually abandoned.

VIETCONG Popular term for Communist insurgents operating in South Vietnam. See National Liberation Front of South Vietnam.

VIETMINH Formally known as the Vietnamese Independence League, a broad coalition of political factions, radical and moderate, organized and directed by Communists to overcome foreign rule and establish Vietnamese independence.

VIETNAMIZATION The Nixon administration's policy of building up the South Vietnamese army so it could take on a greater share of the fighting while gradually reducing the American military presence in Vietnam.

SELECTED BIBLIOGRAPHY

Alterman, Eric. *When Presidents Lie: A History of Official Deception and Its Consequences.* New York: Penguin Books, 2005.

Appy, Christian. *Working Class War: American Combat Soldiers and Vietnam.* Chapel Hill: University of North Carolina Press, 1993.

Arendt, Hannah. *Crises of the Republic.* San Diego: Harcourt Brace, 1972.

Asprey, Robert B. *War in the Shadows: The Guerrilla in History,* Vol. 1. New York: Doubleday, 1975.

Becker, Elizabeth. *America's Vietnam War: A Narrative History.* New York: Clarion Books, 1992.

Caputo, Philip. *A Rumor of War.* New York: Henry Holt, 1996.

Chomsky, Noam. *At War with Asia.* New York: Pantheon Books/Random House, 1970.

Dallek, Robert. *Lyndon B. Johnson: Portrait of a President.* New York: Oxford University Press, 2005.

———. *Nixon and Kissinger: Partners in Power.* New York: HarperCollins, 2007.

Dommen, Arthur J. *The Indochinese Experience of the French and the Americans: Nationalism and Communism in Cambodia, Laos, and Vietnam.* Bloomington: Indiana University Press, 2002.

Duiker, William J. *Ho Chi Minh: A Life.* New York: Hyperion, 2000.

———. *Sacred War: Nationalism and Revolution in a Divided Vietnam.* New York: McGraw Hill, 1995.

Fitzgerald, Frances. *Fire in the Lake: The Vietnamese and the Americans in Vietnam.* Boston: Little, Brown, 1972.

Hagopian, Patrick. *The Vietnam War in American Memory: Veterans, Memorials, and the Politics of Healing.* Amherst: University of Massachusetts Press, 2009.

Halberstam, David. *The Best and the Brightest.* New York: Ballantine Books, 1992.

Haldeman, H. R., with Joseph DiMona. *The Ends of Power.* New York: Dell, 1978.

Herr, Michael. *Dispatches*. New York: Vintage Books, 1991.

Hersh, Seymour M. *The Price of Power: Kissinger in the Nixon White House*. New York: Summit Books, 1983.

Ho Chi Minh. *Selected Writings 1920–1969*. Honolulu: University Press of the Pacific, 2001. First published 1973 by Foreign Languages Publishing House, Hanoi.

Hunt, Andrew W. *The Turning: A History of Vietnam Veterans Against the War*. New York: NYU Press, 2001.

Jones, Howard. *Death of a Generation: How the Assassination of Diem and JFK Prolonged the Vietnam War*. New York: Oxford University Press, 2003.

Kaku, Michio, and Daniel Axelrod. *To Win a Nuclear War: The Pentagon's Secret War Plans*. Boston: South End Press, 1999.

Karnow, Stanley. *Vietnam: A History*. 2nd ed. New York: Penguin Books, 1997.

Langer, Howard. *The Vietnam War: An Encyclopedia of Quotations*. Westport, CT: Greenwood Press, 2006.

Lawrence, Mark Atwood. *The Vietnam War: A Concise International History*. New York: Oxford University Press, 2008.

Lockard, Craig. *Southeast Asia in World History*. New York: Oxford University Press, 2009.

McCarthy, Mary. *Vietnam*. New York: Harcourt Brace & World, 1967.

MacKenzie, G. Calvin, and Robert Weisbrot. *The Liberal Hour: Washington and the Politics of Change in the 1960s*. New York: Penguin, 2008.

McNamara, Robert S. *In Retrospect: The Tragedy and Lessons of Vietnam*. New York: Vintage Books, 1996.

——— et al. *Argument without End: In Search of Answers to the Vietnam Tragedy*. New York: PublicAffairs, 2000.

Race, Jeffrey. *War Comes to Long An: Revolutionary Conflict in a Vietnamese Province*. Berkeley: University of California Press, 1972.

Reeves, Richard. *President Nixon: Alone in the White House*. New York: Simon & Schuster, 2001.

Reporting Vietnam: American Journalism 1959–1975. New York: Library of America, 2000.

Ruane, Kevin. *War and Revolution in Vietnam, 1930–75*. New York: Routledge, 1998.

Schell, Jonathan. *The Real War*. New York: Pantheon Books, 1988.

Schmitz, David F. *The Tet Offensive: Politics, War, and Public Opinion.* Lanham, MD: Rowman & Littlefield, 2005.

Sheehan, Neil. *A Bright Shining Lie: John Paul Vann and America in Vietnam.* New York: Vintage Books, 1989.

Solomon, Eugene. *Lies and Deceits.* New York: Universe, 2010.

Spector, Ronald. *After Tet: The Bloodiest Year in Vietnam.* New York: Vintage, 1993.

Thomas, G. Scott. *A New World to Be Won: John Kennedy, Richard Nixon, and the Tumultuous World of 1960.* New York: Praeger, 2011.

Tirman, John. *The Deaths of Others: The Fate of Civilians in America's Wars.* New York: Oxford University Press, 2011.

Trullinger, James W. *Village at War: An Account of Conflict in Vietnam.* Stanford, CA: Stanford University Press, 1980.

Wiest, Andrew, and Michael Doidge, eds. *Triumph Revisited: Historians Battle for the Vietnam War.* New York: Routledge, 2010.

Young, Marilyn B. *The Vietnam Wars: 1945–1990.* New York: Harper, 1991.

PICTURE CREDITS

Associated Press: 27, 28, 49, 62, 65, 67, 95, 102

AP Photo/Malcolm Browne: 58

AP Photo/Horst Faas: vi, 63

AP Photo/FOW: 4

AP Photo/Kim Ki Sam: 8

AP Photo/Frances Stammer: 119

AP Photo/Nick Ut: 80

AP Photo/Sal Veder: 116

AP Photo/Evan Vucci: 125

Corbis/Bettmann/AP Images: 32, 44, 51, 75, 109, 110

Evans Chan: 9, 10 (lower), 16, 120, 131, 135

Getty/Bettmann: 40

Getty/LIFE Picture collection/John Dominis: 11

Getty/Keystone-France: 25

Getty/Hutton Archive/Keystone: 36

Library of Congress: 14, 55, 57, 59, 77, 82, 86, 89, 105, 108

National Archives: 23, 78, 81, 84, 90

Minnesota Historical Society: 87

University of Wisconsin-Madison Collection: 88

Wikipedia/Creative Commons: ii, 2, 41, 66, 92, 122, 123, 124, 127, 128

Wikipedia/public domain: 7, 10 (upper), 12, 18, 20, 21, 22, 30, 33, 34, 37, 38, 45, 47, 52, 54, 69, 71, 72, 91, 94, 97, 98, 99, 103, 106, 107, 113, 115, 117, 118

INDEX

Page numbers in *italics* refer to illustrations.